The Fly Fisher's Illustrated Dictionary

Books by Darrel Martin

Micropatterns
Fly-Tying Methods
The Fly Fisher's Illustrated Dictionary

The Fly Fisher's Illustrated Dictionary

Darrel Martin

Foreword by Ted Leeson

The Lyons Press

Design by Compset Inc.

Printed in the United States of America

10 9 8 7 6 5 4 3 2 1

Library of Congress Cataloging-in-Publication Data is
available on file.

For Muriel Estelle Martin

Contents

Foreword

The language of fly fishing, like fishing itself, is an amalgam of the ancient and modern. As angling has changed over the course of centuries, so have the words used by fly fishers to describe what they do. The appropriation of a new tying material, an innovation in tackle or technique, the development of a new fly design—each has shaped the vocabulary of the sport, enlarging or revising its store of words. As a result, the terminology of fly fishing has been nothing if not restless and dynamic. This is hardly a coincidence. The language of angling has always been a part of the language of the larger culture, rooted first in the names of animals and plants; in the crafts of spinning, weaving, needle-making, and woodworking; and more recently in aquatic biology, entomology, and engineering. And language of the larger culture has itself never stood still.

This accumulation of words, layer upon layer—some persisting through time, others abandoned or replaced or added—ultimately constitutes a kind of archaeological record, a cross-sectional history of fly fishing that encapsulates both continuity and change. And I can think of no one better qualified to sort through and explain this record than Darrel Martin, one of fly fishing's most knowledgeable authorities. Formerly a teacher of Old and Middle English literature, Darrel brings to his task the historian's sense of relentless curiosity, the scholar's love of words, and the antiquarian's delight in details. The result is a fascinating dictionary that explains the vocabulary and nomenclature of fly fishing, both historical and modern. You will find here not only discussions of hooks and dressing materials, fly styles and proportions, fishing tackle and methods, but also useful information about aquatic entomology, avian anatomy, and a host of other matters that pertain to fly fishing and fly tying. Many of the entries are supplemented by photographs and many others by the author's superb illustrations.

Such a book is a welcome addition to any angler's library. *The Fly Fisher's Illustrated Dictionary* is a valuable aid in clarifying the specialized terminology and the vocabulary of concepts that surround fishing with the artificial fly. It is an absolutely indispensable reference for those who wish to read and understand the angling literature of centuries past. And it serves the needs of anyone who believes that being a more knowledgeable fly fisher is being a better one. But beyond its practical application, this volume is simply and wonderfully interesting.

—Ted Leeson

Acknowledgments

To Nick Lyons, whose fondness for words made this possible. To Richard Westerfield for his enthusiasm. To John and Judith Head, who shared their book stacks. To Marvin Nolte for his talents and patterns caught in these pages. To John Betts, whose thoughtful insights have made this dictionary and my angling life much richer. To Rick Hafele for his friendship and entomological knowledge. And to Sandra, my wife, who proofed so many pages. No single writer has sufficient *oyl*.

Introduction

*As for this little Treatise, many persons have con-
tributed much Oyl to its Lamp.*

—James Chetham
The Angler's Vade Mecum (third edition, 1700)

Samuel Johnson, that literary dictator of the eighteenth
century, defined the lexicographer as "a writer of dictio-
naries, a harmless drudge." Although he noted that "fly
fishing may be a very pleasant amusement," he compared angling to "a stick and string, with a worm at one
end and a fool at the other." But even fools and harmless
drudges can find "very pleasant amusement" in the *language* of fly fishing.

Words have sounds and tales and histories. Some
words have charming tales, like *Isabella* and *sneck*.
Some have delightful sounds, like *snood* and *sniggle*.
And some reveal histories, like *bloa* and *loop-rod*.

Like a trout in August, this modest dictionary is selective. I have included terms that I enjoy and deliber-
ately omitted terms that are readily available in common
sources. Such a selective and limited dictionary will always be judged by what is included and what is omitted.
No single text could contain all angling words and all
their histories.

This dictionary, which includes angling and fly-tying terms, attempts to clarify many antique and obscure words found in past and present angling writing. Entomological terms, often the handmaiden to fly tying, are also included. A few angling terms, not directly related to fly fishing per se, have been included because of what they reveal. Some included terms are still ambiguous and problematic. Others have multiple meanings and a few are merely strange. It is also important to recognize that occasionally a word may have various meanings and that a scientific term may be endowed with a nontechnical meaning or even an erroneous meaning. Anything long used, even in error, may become an accepted standard. The study of angling terms is freighted with pleasures and problems. I have tried, like Samuel Johnson, to avoid most "wild blunders and risible absurdities."

The language of fly fishing is a specialized imagery of a particular activity. In England, the Anglo-Saxon angler called the common trout a *sceota*, a "shooter" or "darter" of the currents. It was not until the fifteenth century that the *shooter* or *darter* became the Norman *trout* (late Old English *truht* from late Latin *tructa*). And the word *trout* originally came from the Greek *troktes,* "the gnawer" (from *trogein*, to gnaw). Thus the quick, darting fish became the fish that bites. I like to think that this is a reference to the rise and strike of the trout. In any case, like the river itself, the current of language constantly flows and changes.

A lexicon should be clear and certain. It gathers the etymologies, the cognates, the genesis, and, sometimes, even the social history of a word. Some words are clear while others remain cloudy. Some terms, through growth and decay, have been transformed to mean their opposite. Some terms have become more specific, while others have become more general. Some have risen on the acceptance scale, while others have sunk. Some are natives; others, naturalized foreigners. Words reveal the development of fly fishing in different lands at different times. For some years I have had a beat on the Fullerton water of the Anton and the river Test in southern England. Roman coins, Anglo-Saxon buckles, and medieval trinkets are all found in its waters and on its banks. Rivers, like angling itself, seem to gather history.

This dictionary is a modern medieval pony: a translator of antique angling books and a reference for many angling topics. Fly fishing, one of the oldest field sports, is a meandering stream. We capture those words that readily rise, and—with a subtle, sunk line—catch a few that are strange and wondrous. This dictionary is the spindrift of centuries of fly fishing.

Special note: All significant quotes have cited sources. The semicolon entry usually indicates the various meanings or shades of meaning. Any historical lexicon must rely greatly on *The Oxford English Dictionary*, in various editions, including *The Shorter Oxford English Dictionary on Historical Principles*, third edition, 1973. References to the Oxford English Dictionary are abbreviated throughout as *OED*. Consult the bibliography for complete entries of works cited.

The Fly Fisher's
Illustrated Dictionary

Advanced wing

A wing mounted to slope *over* and *beyond* the hook eye, usually at an angle of 45 degrees, rather than over the body or erect. Such wings may be either single or divided. "Originally this method of winging was applied only to the Mole Fly, but in recent years its use has been extended to some other patterns" (A. Courtney Williams, *A Dictionary of Trout Flies* [1982]). Advanced wings appear on several French patterns, such as the *Grisette, Pont l'Evêque,* and *Pont Audemer.* Jean-Paul Pequegnot, in *French Fishing Flies* (1987), describes the unusual float attitude of the tailless, advanced-wing patterns: "For the majority of the Norman anglers, the original had no tails. Such a fly assumes a very unusual posture on the water, the hook penetrating the surface so that the fly is suspended by the hackle collar. The wings are then very visible and the leader forms a little aerial bridge, the value of which is certain and in which I believe." The advanced wings resist casting pressure and offer the angler and trout an unobstructed wing silhouette.

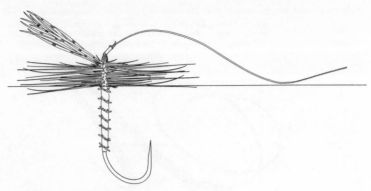

Advanced wing fly and float attitude

Aelianus (Aelian), Claudius

A Roman writer and teacher of rhetoric who wrote in
Greek and lived in Rome in the late second and early
third centuries A.D. William Radcliffe, in *Fishing from
the Earliest Times* (1974), dates Aelianus from 170 to
230 A.D. Aelianus, known as "the Sophist," was a teacher
of rhetoric in Rome during the second century A.D. His
surviving works include *De Natura Animalium,* a copi-
ous collection of curiosities of life, including the first explicit reference to fly fishing and an artificial fly pattern
(Book XV, Section I). Although John Waller Hills, in *A
History of Fly Fishing for Trout* (1971), quickly dis-
misses the brief entry as "interesting rather than important," Aelianus, who was not an angler and who based his
facts on hearsay, does give us the first river (the Astraeus), the first insect (the Hipporus), and the first re-
corded artificial fly. The angling gear, a short, 6-foot rod
and horsehair line, suggests dapping. Aelianus notes that
"Between Beroea (Beria) and Thessalonica there flows a
river called the Astraeus." The river has been variously
identified as the Aliakmon, the Axios, the Kotiha, and the
Arapitsa. The Astraeus—sometimes identified as the *Astraeus flumen* and the *Aistraios F?* (*Nordliches Hellas,*

Map of the Astraeus River (*Ancient Greece,* Baldwin & Gradock, 1829)

Berlin, 1871)—does appear on several ancient maps in ambiguous or vague locations. Often, the older the map, the more doubtful the map. The veracity of mapped locations is contested. One such map, which appears above, identifies the Astraeus River (the modern Edessaios, Vodhas?) near Edessa. *This* Astraeus flows only to Yannitsa, the ancient lake at Pella, and not, as Aelianus describes, "between Beroea (Beria) and Thessalonica." It is the Ludias River that completes the journey.

Conrad Voss Bark, in *A History of Fly Fishing* (1992), insists that "Aelian flounders when he tries to describe the fly." Actually, the description and details are remarkably specific though enigmatic. The Hipporus has the color of a wasp and the *size* and *buzz* of a bee. It has been variously identified as an aquatic soldier fly, a grasshopper, a caddis, and a mayfly. Like the river location, Hipporus is a pile of perhaps.

Aelianus gives us the first recipe in fly tying: "They wrap the hook in scarlet wool, and to the wool they attach two feathers that grow beneath a cock's wattles and are the colour of wax." There is no indication as to *how* the pattern was tied. The hackles could have been palmered or winged, either erect (like a mayfly) or down (like a caddis or Diptera). "Two feathers," however, suggest two wings, perhaps reverse mounted, rather than body or shoulder hackles.

Aerobic
A habitat, such as a stream or lake, with free and available oxygen.

Aftershaft
The small, soft undershaft or underfeather directly beneath and attached to another feather. The aftershaft is also called the *hyporachis,* the insulating accessory plume connected to the underside base of a feather. The term aftershaft and the synonym *hyporachis* should be restricted to the auxiliary shaft only. The aftershaft has also been called an accessory plume, the afterfeather, or *hypoptile (hypoptilum).* The term afterfeather is a direct translation of the German term, *afterfeder,* introduced by Studer in 1878.

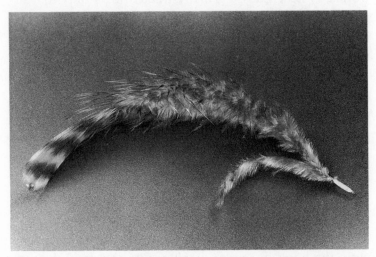

The short, soft aftershaft feather attached to the concave or underside of a contour feather

The aftershaft or afterfeather consists of an aftershaft *(hyporachis)* with its own aftervanes *(hypovexillum)*. The aftershaft is a soft feather that varies in type. In grouse, quail, and pheasant, the aftershaft is long and narrow with relatively short barbs. In the turkey, the aftershaft is often oval or elliptical with long, fine barbs that are one-third to two-thirds the length of the main vane. In ducks, the aftershaft is very short with no central stem or *hyporachis.*

AFTMA line designations

In 1961, the American Fishing Tackle Manufacturers Association (AFTMA; now the American Sportsfishing Association, or ASA) established a numerical line-rating system that replaced the older letter-designation system. The older silk line system used letters (such as HCH) to indicate the line diameter and taper. Because of the uniformity of the material (silk) and manufacturing methods, the letter diameter, ranging from *A* (0.060") to *I* (0.20"), indicated line weight. With the advent of synthetic lines, however, the letter-diameter designation became meaningless. The various materials, cores, finishes, and braids created different line weights for a particular diameter. AFTMA chose a new standard based on the weight of the first 30 feet of fly line (an assumed aerialized length) exclusive of the level tip. This first 30 feet of line should "load" but not "collapse" the rod. The weight unit is based on grains: 437½ grains = 1 ounce. Fly lines range from a 1-weight (60 grains) to a 12-weight (380 grains). After all, a fly rod casts the weight rather than the diameter of a line. Thus, any rod that responds to 30 feet of 140 grains of line (no matter what the material or taper) is a 5-weight rod. Letters identify the various line tapers and type: DT = double taper, WF = weight forward, ST = shooting taper, L = level, F = floating, S = sinking, and I = intermediate. Modern fly lines have a core covered with a polyvinal chloride (PVC) taper. Within the PVC taper may be hollow glass microspheres (floating lines) or various density-compensating additives (sinking lines). Variations in the additives account for the differences in fly lines. The scale is now extrapolated to extend from 0 line weight to a 15 line weight. See also *Silk line designations.*

Note: The industry standard includes line weights 1 through 12. Line weights beyond (and even within) the industry standard may vary according to the manufacturer. The Cortland Line Company indicates that for each line weight heavier than 12, add 50 grains to the previous weight. According to Scientific Anglers, a 13-weight line is 450 grains, a 14-weight line, 500 grains, and a 15-weight line, 550 grains, with tolerances of 15 grains plus or minus for each line weight. Sage, the only major company at present producing an 0-weight rod and line, indicates that the 0-weight line is 55 grains with manufacturing tolerance of 52 to 58.

The AFTMA fly line standard

Line Weight	Grain Weight	Manufacturing Tolerances
1	60	54–66
2	80	74–86
3	100	94–106
4	120	114–126
5	140	134–146
6	160	152–168
7	185	177–193
8	210	202–218
9	240	230–250
10	280	270–290
11	330	318–342
12	380	368–392

Amadou

A pale gray or gray-brown parasitic "hoof fungus," *Fomes fomentarius* or *Ungulina fomentaria,* that grows on beech, poplar, oak, and lime trees. Amadou effectively dries fly patterns, especially cul-de-canard patterns. The term *amadou,* from the French, means "lover," owing to "its quick kindling" *(OED).* G. W. Maunsell, in *The Fisherman's Vode Mecum* (1952), notes that the name *Amadou, Fomes (Polyporus) igniarius,* "is said to be derived from the Latin *ad manum dulce* (soft to the hands)." Originally amadou was used as a styptic agent in ancient surgery and as a tinder when mixed with potassium nitrate (saltpeter). Eric Taverner offers a different definition: "The flint of the holster-pistol was once wrapped in a slip of amadou; hence its name, *amadou*, the French for tinder." Before the advent of modern flotants and desiccants, amadou was used to dry floating flies. G. E. M. Skues's *The Way of a Trout with a Fly* (1935) concludes with an advertisement, an ovation on amadou: "Dry fly men who know what is good for them use it for drying flies.

A cross-section of harvested amadou

Salmon-fly anglers are going to find it first-rate for the purpose of drying and preserving their salmon flies. Wet and mangled May flies washed and then dried with it resume their pristine youth and beauty. Amadou quadruples the life of an ordinary May fly." At present, most amadou comes from Romania, Lithuania, and Bohemia. Slices of the raw fungus are dropped into solution, after which they are drained and pounded with a wooden mallet to make them soft and supple. Hats, vests, table mats, and other products are still made from amadou.

Anadromous
Ascending from the sea for reproduction; said of fish, such as salmon and steelhead, that migrate annually into fresh water for reproduction. Conversely, fish that migrate from fresh water to the sea to spawn are called *catadromous*.

Anaerobic
A habitat without free oxygen, such as occurs in the deep (profundal) areas of lakes.

Anastomosed
The condensed wing vein network; the "coming together" or channeled vein connections, said of insect wings.

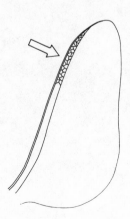

Anastomosed

Apolysis

The separation, but not the casting off, of the larval integument from the pupal integument. The actual shedding of the larval integument is called *ecdysis*.

Arm

Fastening the hook to the line. "To arm . . . with necessary appendages (1534). 'First you must arm your hook,' Walton" *(OED)*. ". . . Take your Silk with Right, and twisting it betwixt the Finger and Thumb of that Hand, the Dubbing will spin it self about the Silk, which, when it has done, whip it about the armed Hook backward, till you come to the setting on of the Wings . . ." (James Chetham, *The Angler's Vade Mecum* [1700]). "For setting the hook, or more scientifically speaking, *arming it,* use strong but small silk, lightly waxed with shoemaker's wax; and lay the hair on the inside of the hook, for if it be on the outside, the silk will fret and cut it asunder" (Thomas Best, *The Art of Angling* [1822]). "For fixing the hook to the gut, grass, or hair, which is termed *arming* or *whipping,* use small but strong silk. . . ." (James Rennie, *Alphabet of Angling* [1849]). According to Rennie, arming is also called whipping and "Provincially, *whooping or Ooping.*" J. March, in *The Jolly Angler* (1842), offers explicit directions on arming with the sense of protection: "Then wind it round the end of the shank of the hook (taking the gut in with it) two or three times; then twice around the gut without the hook, so as the silk may lie between the gut and the extremity of the inside of the shank of the hook, to prevent its cutting the gut; this is called the arming." Note that this description means to furnish with a protective covering, a meaning dating from Middle English.

The term "arming" seldom appears in contemporary tying books. ". . . It is a good plan to 'arm' the gut against the hook shank by taking a couple of turns alternately round the gut and then around gut and shank together" (T. R. Henn, *Practical Fly-Tying* [1950]). The thread arms or protects the gut from the hook. "To arm" also means to add the "necessary appendages," such as to attach a gut line to a hook.

Astraeus

According to Claudius Aelianus, a river in ancient Macedonia where fly fishing was practiced. The actual location of the Astraeus is a classical angling conundrum. For further information on the river and reference, see *Aelianus, Claudius.*

Badger

A cream, silver, golden (etc.) feather with a black center; a cape of badger feathers; a badger feather may have a black list or edge. The term probably comes from the Old English *broc(k)*, a reference to the light and dark fur of a badger. E. Muller suggests that the term *badger* (from *badge* plus *-ard*) is derived from the reference to the white badge mark on the animal's forehead. Earlier names for the animal were *brock* (appears in Middle English, c. 1230) and *bauson*.

Bank designation

Older angling books usually define river banks in the following manner: *When facing downstream,* the right bank of a river is on the right side and the left bank is on the left side. The bottom of the channel is known as the streambed or "ground;" the sides are the banks. "Face down stream. The right bank is on your right. The left bank is on your left" (G. W. Maunsell, *The Fisherman's Vade Mecum* [1952]). The U.S. Environmental Protec-

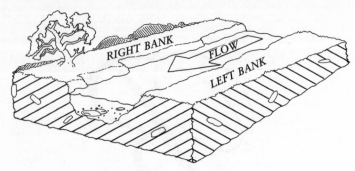

Traditional bank designation

tion Agency (EPA) defines the banks looking downstream. Modern agency protocol may define the banks differently. Bank orientation may be defined in terms of the fish, i.e., facing upstream, with the right bank on the right side and the left bank on the left side.

Barb (noun)
(1) The lateral feather fiber branching from the rachis or shaft. See *Feather (nomenclature)*. (2) The elevated cut on a top of the hook point immediately behind the point.

Barb (verb)
"To shave or trim, to clip or mow," 1483 *(OED)*. Even Charles Cotton endorsed trimmed hackle barbs: " . . . We have a Great Hackle, the body black, and wrapped with a red feather of a Capon untrimmed; that is, the whole length of the hackle staring out; for we sometimes barb the Hackle-feather short all over; sometimes barb it only a little, and sometimes barb it close underneath, leaving the whole length of the feather on the top, or back of the flie, which makes it swim better, and, as occasion serves, kills very great fish" (Izaak Walton, *The Complete Angler* [1766]). See also *Barb (noun)* and *Witter.*

Barbicel

On a feather, the hook or clawlike projection of the barbule. See *Feather (nomenclature)*.

Barbless hook

A hook manufactured without a barb or a hook with the barb flattened or removed. Barbless hooks were probably available before 1890. Mary Orvis Marbury, in *Favorite Flies and Their Histories* (1892), noted that "We would like to show some of the curiosities in novel-shaped hooks that have come to us: some with the barb on the outside of the hook; and some with no barb at all. . . ."

An unusual hook was Allcock's Jamison Barbless Hook, produced in 1924. This hook received both U.S. and U.K. patents. The large loop-bend probably prevented effective penetration and hold. Compare Mustad 3257B.

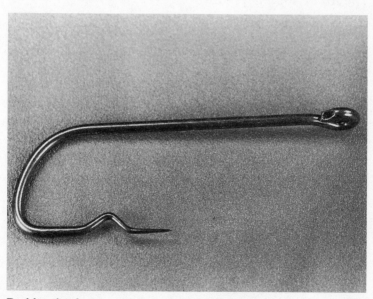

Barbless hook

Barbule
On a feather, the lateral projection of the barb; the interlaced webbing. See *Feather (nomenclature)*.

Basket wings
See *Halford wings*.

Bawk (line making)
A knot or kink in a horsehair fly line. "A knot in a hair or link" (Thomas Best, *The Art of Angling* [1822]).

Beard, berde
The barb of a hook. See *Barb (noun)*.

Beard hackle
A false hackle; a bundle of hackle barbs mounted beneath the hook and not conventionally wound.

Bed (line making)
"Hairs bed well when they twist kindly" (Thomas Best, *The Art of Angling* [1822]).

Bedding
"The body of an artificial fly" (Thomas Best, *The Art of Angling* [1822]).

Bent-hackle fly
An unusual fly-pattern design so defined by Datus Proper in *What the Trout Said* (1982). "A large, soft hackle—such as a dyed French Partridge—is wound on shiny-side forward, supported by a small, stiff cock's hackle out of sight behind the main hackle. The function of the stiff hackle is purely mechanical; it strengthens the middle of the soft hackle, while the soft tips bend backwards around the point of the hook. The fly floats on the bends of the soft hackle fibers. Nothing at all penetrates the surface film, something difficult to achieve with any other pattern. A good fly flotant helps to keep the soft

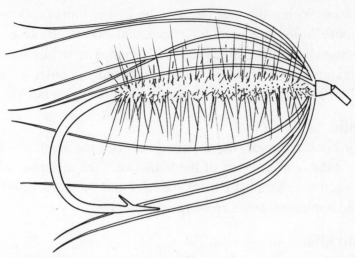

Bent-hackle fly

fibers from soaking up water instantly. At best, however, the bent-hackle fly is suitable for only a few casts over a rising fish—but that should be enough." This design, decades old, duplicates the French dry flies that wear palmer hackles that support long, soft shoulder hackles. One such pattern, the *Plumeaux* (Feather Duster), sports a long-barbed, yellow mallard breast feather supported by reddish brown hackles. See *French Fishing Flies* (1987) by Jean-Paul Pequegnot for other examples.

Benthic
An adjective describing the flora or fauna inhabiting or associated with the bottom or substratum of a body of water; bottom dwelling.

Biot
The leading lateral barb of a goose quill; the stiff and rapidly tapering barb, usually on the leading edge of a primary feather; such a barb on any bird's feather. Biots are often used for nymph tails, antenna, legs, and wing

cases. Within the past decade, the longer biots (such as goose biots) are used for segmented bodies. Biots are somewhat brittle, stiff, and readily bent. The term, origin unknown, appears to be modern, especially popular since the 1980s, and does not appear in the older tying books.

Bite

In hook parlance, the distance between the hook point and the rearmost part of the hook bend; the distance between the rearmost part of the heel and the hook point; the hook *throat*. See *Hook (nomenclature)*.

Bivisible

Term credited to Edward Ringwood Hewitt in *Telling on the Trout* (1926). The Bivisible consists of a double palmer, usually with a forward, light-colored, or white face hackle: "The white wisp enables the angler to see the fly readily, hence the name I gave it 'Bivisible' because I can see it and the trout can see it" (Hewitt, quoted by Harold Smedley in *Fly Patterns and Their Origins* [1950]). Such patterns are designed to improve the visibility of the fly—especially small, dark patterns in low light—to both trout and angler.

Bloa

In fly tying, the color blue-gray or comparable color. "This is a North-country word, and as I am told, signifies a colour resembling that of a Mole's back, which has a bluish gloss" (Izaak Walton and Charles Cotton, *The Complete Angler* [1766], Number II, Appendix). "Bloa, or Blea, a North-country word, signifying the colour of the clouds. Blea seems generally significant of cold" (John Jackson, *The Practical Fly-Fisher* [1899]). "Pertaining to the color of the clouds, leaden, bluish purple, or pale blue, was used to mean dun colored" and "the color of the lowery clouds of a threatening sky" (Harold

Smedley, *Fly Patterns and Their Origins* [1950]). The blae of the Scottish patterns and the bloa of the Yorkshire patterns; compare Old Norse *blar,* bluish black, and *blautr,* soaked or wet; term used in such fly patterns as the Bloa and Red, and Blae and Silver.

Blow line

"A fishing line of the lightest floss silk, used with the living fly" *(OED)*. "The line is composed of the lightest, loosest, and airiest floss silk—so web-like that the least puff of wind will drive it before it. Light and loose as it is, it has abundant strength. The rod used generally resembles the mast of a fishing smack, being of the lightest cane, but as long as can be obtained or worked. It generally runs to nineteen or twenty feet, and often beyond that. As a foot-line or cast, there is some two feet or more of very fine gut, and a hook to match. On this hook is impaled a live May fly. . . . The angler then chooses the bank of the stream whence the wind is blowing, and walks up the bank; when he sees a good fish, he turns his back to the wind, faces the fish, lets out line enough just to clear the ground, holds the rod perfectly upright, and allows the wind to take the line out over the river, which, if but a very moderate breeze is on, it will do easily. When it is bellied out half way or three parts across the stream, judging his distance carefully, the angler slowly lowers the point of the rod, so that if he has measured his distance pretty rightly the fly will light where or whereabouts the fish is rising, and a little above it of course; and as the fly can be lowered on to the water *au naturel* like thistledown, and by the skillful working of the rod point can be made even to skip or flutter up and down on the surface like a natural insect. . . ." (Francis Francis, *A Book on Angling* [1876]). The blow line is also used with the artificial fly, especially a buzz or palmer pattern. See *Dapping*.

Bobbin

In fly tying, the bobbin holds the thread spool. The weight of the tool eliminates the need for half hitches during tying. Bobbin features include (1) rigid spool arms to prevent twisting, (2) adequate weight for thread tension, (3) small-diameter tube for precise thread control, (4) adjustable spool tension and smooth thread flow, (5) smooth tube lips to prevent thread fraying or breaking, (6) alignment of tube and spool to lessen wax removal, (7) comfortable balance and hand conformity, (8) minimal length for working beneath the vise head, and (9) adequate spool size or spool range.

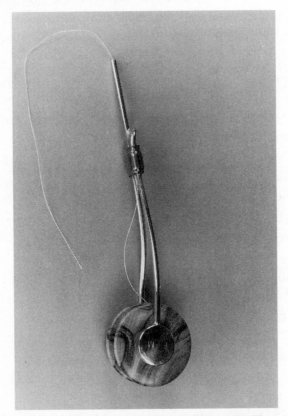

Standard *midge bobbin* made by Frank Matarelli. The moderate offset of tube and spool fits the hand and minimizes wax buildup.

Bob fly

The top dropper; the top fly when two or more flies are mounted to the same cast or leader. "Its function is to 'bob' or skate on or along the surface" (A. Courtney Williams, *A Dictionary of Trout Flies* [1982]). "The collar of gut we are to use should be made of six or eight links, and three flies may be put at intervals of two links apart, so that we shall have three or perhaps four links between the fly nearest the line, or as it is commonly called, the bob fly" (H. C. Cutcliffe, *The Art of Trout Fishing on Rapid Streams* [1863]). See *Stretcher.*

Bottom or ground fishing

"To angle near, or on the bottom of the river; so called to distinguish it from fly-fishing" (J. March, *The Jolly Angler* [1842]). This definition infers that fly fishing is done on or near the surface. Modern weighted lines and patterns, however, do permit bottom fly fishing.

Budget

See *Magazine.*

Bulla

The "bubble node" or "blister" usually found midway along the subcostal vein of an insect wing.

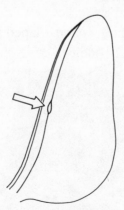

Wing bulla. Wing drawing is greatly simplified.

Bullet head

In fly tying, a method popularized by Keith Fulsher's Thunder Creek streamer series for forming a head or body by reversing bundled hair or fibers. Usually, a bullet head tool, also called a hair compressor, compresses the hairs during tying. The hairs may completely encircle the hook shank or may be drawn on top of the hook shank for positioning.

This bullet-head tool, made by Griffin Enterprises, compresses reversed hair, creating a sleek "bullet" head. The tool forms heads for adult grasshoppers and stoneflies as well as plump bodies for beetles and spiders.

Burnisher, tinsel

In fly tying, a small, spoon-shaped tool that polishes and smoothes tinsel fly bodies.

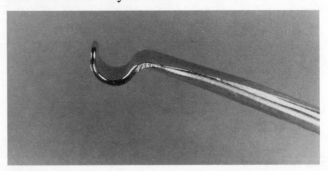

Modern Matarelli tinsel burnisher

Buzz

A palmered pattern is a buzz pattern. "A hackled fly is sometimes described as being tied 'buzz' " (A. Courtney Williams, *A Dictionary of Trout Flies* [1982]). "The fashion of the day is to call this kind of hackle [Palmer Hackle], buzz" and "These hackle or buzz flies are much more in use than winged flies" (T. C. Hofland, *The British Angler's Manual* [1838, first edition]). "What is called the buzz form, is an intended imitation of the natural fly struggling and half drowned" ("Ephemera" [Edward Fitzgibbon], *A Handbook of Angling* [1848]). According to Harold Smedley, in *Fly Patterns and Their Origins* (1950), "Seth Green in 1879, wrote that a 'buzz' was made with 'the hackle standing out the whole length of the body.' " The effect of a buzz or bush hackle and a fluttering insect may sometimes appear similar to the trout. Some anglers believed that palmers were often taken for emerging sedges. A hackle, especially a variegated hackle, might suggest movement. The banded grizzly-point wings and variegated hackle of an Adams, for example, may suggest the vibrant fluttering of an insect attempting to fly. G. E. M. Skues, in *The Way of a Trout with a Fly* (1935), believed that the hackle of a buzz pattern actually imitated the appearance of transparent wings: ". . . A good sharp cock's hackle with the light through it is nothing but sheer sparkle. It has no appearance of solidity at all. It may merely give an effect of translucency to the wings."

Buzzer

The Chironomid (U.K.); see *Chironomid.*

Cad

The cod-bait, cadbate, corbait (Irish), cadis, cadiss (Thomas Best, *The Art of Angling* [1822]), cod-worm, caddis, sedge, or *Tricoptera*; the term *cadew*, a variant of caddis, is of unknown origin, chiefly dialect and dated 1668 in reference to the cased Tricoptera *(OED)*. "Cad, chiefly dial. 1651, variation of caddis; called more fully cod-bait, 1626" *(OED)*. "Yellow may fly, or Cadow. This is the most important fly for Trout fishing of any, because at this period the Trout is in its greatest perfection; it is bred from the cad-worm, and is found in considerable numbers at the sides of most small gravelly rivers, on bushes which overhang the water; to which places they resort when they change from their chrysalis state" (Charles Bowlker, *The Art of Angling* [1839]). Thomas Best, in *The Art of Angling* (1822) describes the "cadiss": "A large four-winged fly, of a buff colour as its wings . . . it is bred from the cod-bait, a curious little insect: while in the state of a grub it is greatly to be admired, the outside husk that it lives in, being curiously wrought with gravel or sand." James Chetham notes in *The Angler's Vade Mecum* (1700) that the best caddis are those that live in a "fine gravelly Case or Husk" and are "yellow when ripe." See *Caddis*.

Caddis

The sedge or Trichoptera; from the Old French *cadas,* meaning "silk floss" with reference to the caddis case appearance; the Middle English *cadas* (from the Old French) and *cadace* refer to the coarse, variegated worsted yarn. "Both the caddis or artificial fly and the caddis fly (and caddis worm) derive from caddis, caddice, floss silk, cotton wool, worsted yarn, especially ribbon. . . ." (Eric Partridge, *Origins* [1983]). Also probable origin is the relation to the Greek *cadus,* meaning case, or vessel, perhaps in reference to the cylindrical case of some caddis larva. The larva is called, in the promiscuous angler's argot, such names as rockworm, caseworm, straw-worm (Hofland), and periwinkle.

The tailless adult caddis is dressed in a dull motley. It has four membranous wings. These tent wings, which completely cover the insect's body when at rest, are usually covered with minute hairs or, in some species, scales. The order name, Trichoptera, means "hair-wings" (Greek *tricho* = hair and *ptera* = wing). Caddis have a flopping, fluttering flight. The adults feed on liquid foods—moisture is the most important factor for insect longevity—and will live about one month. They may be found in static and lotic waters. They have a complete metamorphosis, and the aquatic larva, after a year, will pupate. In a manner of speaking, the caddis or sedge is an aquatic silkworm moth.

Pupation lasts about two weeks after the insect seals the case, allowing water entry. The pharate adult (the adult immediately before emergence and still enclosed in the pupal husk) then cuts the case open with mandibles and swims to the surface (in swift water), or crawls out on objects (in calm water), to emerge. The midlegs, or mesotarsi, of the pharate adult are free and formed for subsurface emergence.

The ova are usually laid en masse in the water or on objects; some species enter the water to deposit the eggs. The larval cases, which are cemented with a sticky silk-like saliva, possess a slight negative suspension that helps the larva pull its case along the bottom as it grazes on algae and plant debris. The heavier case construction, of course, occurs in flowing water, whereas the lighter construction occurs in calm water. Most caddis larvae consume various plant life and perform a significant act in the biosystem by producing protein from plants. While it appears that most species hatch during early or late hours of the day, a few species evidently are purely nocturnal in their emergence.

Most adults have lackluster wings and antennae that are two or three times the body length. It is important to note that some species are transformed immediately into fliers as soon as they surface. Others swim and struggle a considerable distance before flight. The struggle of an emerging caddis is perhaps due to the difficulty in breaking the pupal cuticle or increasing wing strength. It is not the act of wing drying. The fine hairs or scales make caddisfly wings water repellent, thereby eliminating the need for drying before flight. On still waters, this flight struggle is quite evident and encourages trout feeding.

Caddis Larva Characteristics
1. Minute antennae
2. Caterpillar-like without wing pads

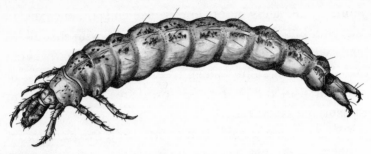

Caddis larva

3. Filamentous gills if present, only on abdominal segments
4. Anal hook on the last abdominal segment
5. Cased (mineral or plant shelter) and uncased (campodeiform) species

Caddis Pupa Characteristics
1. Subsurface emergence upon pupation
2. Antennae nearly body length
3. No anal hook or tail
4. Immediately before emergence, housed in a silk cocoon usually encased in mineral or plant debris

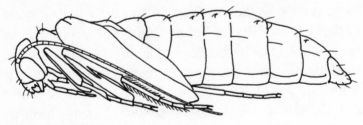

Caddis pupa

Adult Caddis Characteristics
1. Four wings covered with fine hairs or scales
2. Wings swept back and held rooflike over the abdomen
3. Antennae body length or longer
4. A fluttering, floppy flier

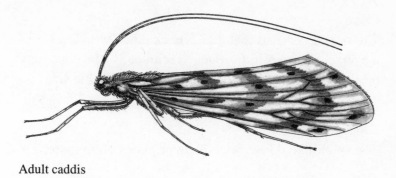

Adult caddis

In fly tying, the imitative elements of the larva are size, color, segmented body, and, on some patterns, case. The imitative elements for the pupa include size, color, legs, wing pad, and silvery emergence sheath. The adult elements often include size, color, tent-wings (which cover the hook bend), and, occasionally, the antennae.

Camlet

Originally, a costly Eastern fabric made from Angora goat hair, especially in the sixteenth and seventeenth centuries; also known as *camelot* (French) and *kamla(t)* or *Kemel* (Arabic for Angora). Although popularly associated with camel hair, "the cloth was never made of camel's hair" (Joseph T. Shipley, *Dictionary of Early English* [1968]). Camlet was later made of mohair, then spun of wool and silk, then wool and linen or cotton. The term, which also has been used for the nap or pile of velvet, dropped from use sometime after 1815. Any various combinations of wool, silk, hair (Angora goat or perhaps true camel), or cotton and linen; a popular dubbing of such material. Angora goat hair woven into a light fabric. "Get pieces of Camlets both Hair and Worsted of all colours" (James Chetham, *The Angler's Vade Mecum* [1700]).

Cape

The dorsal cervical feathers; a neck patch with the hackles attached, used in fly tying. Technically, the cape may be either dry or wet quality, depending on hackle size and degree of webbing.

Carapace

The shieldlike dorsal body plate or plates of an insect.

CDC

Feathers from the duck's derriere; the cul-de-cunard or CDC feathers, which cap and circle the uropygial gland at the base of the upper tail feathers, form a "wick" that transfers oil by capillary action to the duck's bill during preening. There are two distinct types of CDC feathers: the small, stemless "nipple plumes," sometimes called CDC "tufts," and the more abundant, downlike, stemmed feathers. All have kinked and twisted microscopic barbules that trap a "sheath" of air. Because of the embedded oils, these barbules are remarkably water-repellent and buoyant.

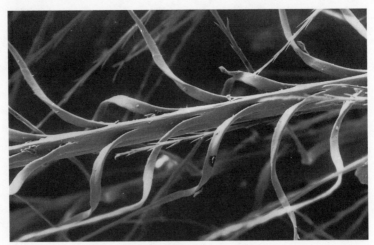

Photo of microscopic CDC barbules

CDC patterns will saturate and sink, but a few brisk backcasts dries them. For more than 100 years in the Swiss Jura, CDC feathers and the pallid yellow or pinkish gland oil have been used in fly tying. About 100 CDC feathers (including the short, stylet "nipple plumes") are harvested from a mature duck, wild or domestic. Natural colors include beige ("Havana"), brown, dun, and black. Most aquatic birds—such as ducks, swans, and geese—have preen-gland feathers. CDC feathers are usually used for body, wings, or hackles of fly patterns. CDC feathers are also known as *croupion de canard,* "the rump of the duck."

Cercus
The "tail" or caudal filaments of an insect located on the tenth abdominal segment; the paired or treble terminal appendages. Technically, the two lateral "tails" are cerci, but the medial "tail" is a medial caudal filament or *telofilum; cerci,* plural.

Cervix
The neck; pertaining to the neck area, or especially the back of the neck of insects.

Chalk stream
A spring creek or stream with waters that are primarily spring fed and filtered through chalk substrata. Chalk streams exist throughout the world. The water usually begins at higher elevations (often as snowmelt and rainfall), filters underground, and emerges at the base of mountains or hills. The stream is generally over a relatively flat plain, such as the river meadows of southern England. The spring water percolates through calcium carbonate (such as chalk or limestone), creating clear, cold, rich water that supports plant growth and abundant

insects. Such water results in well-fed fish, which often rise throughout the day. The Test, the Itchen, the Anton, and the Kennet are famous English chalk streams.

Chalk streams, like all spring creeks, are stable stream habitats, characterized by clear, alkaline water, light penetration (photosynthesis), nearly uniform flow, constant temperatures, gentle gradients, moderate to slow currents, and remarkable weed growth (organic richness). Due to the placid flow, a chalk-stream trout "on the fin" may drift and inspect some distance before accepting or rejecting an insect or fly pattern. Because of the opulent growth of water plants, such rivers may require periodic "mowing" with weed boats, chain or gang scythes, and hand scythes. Excessive weeds can choke a river and cause flooding, erosion, and silting. Ron Wilton, a river-keeper on the Itchen, defines the chalk stream as "a flood under control." Weed cutting maintains the flow and health of the stream. In contrast, a freestone river, or "a slime-stone" river, is primarily fed from tributary surface water (rainfall or snowmelt) that greatly fluctuates during the seasons.

At times, chalk-stream trout may be highly selective. Constant water temperature prolongs hatches so that numerous hatches appear at the same time. The insects, however, are usually restricted. Although you may find minor rapids on chalk streams, they are highly limited or absent, as are the fast-water flies, like clinging mayflies and stoneflies. Instead, there is usually an abundance of smaller crawlers and swimmers. Although large, bushy patterns are sometimes used, chalk-stream patterns are usually small, sparsely hackled, and imitative.

Chalk streams and spring creeks are little affected by rapid snowmelt, thus they may be fished when freestone rivers are unfishable. "The true chalk streams have few tributaries, and are entirely dependent for their supply of water on springs rising at the foot of the chalk downs. These springs in turn are nourished by rainfall. . . " (Kenneth Mansfield, editor, *The Art of Angling* [1960]). The rain, purified by the natural chalk filter, returns to the surface some months later. Water level, therefore, depends primarily on the previous winter's rainfall. Summer rains usually have a minimal effect. When silted through bank erosion or pasture runoff, the streams usually clear within a few hours. Although water levels may fluctuate from season to season, chalk streams seldom flood or become unfishable because of low water. See *Freestone* river.

Chaytor knot
The blood knot, or barrel knot, first described by A. H. Chaytor in *Letters to a Salmonfisher's Son* (1910).

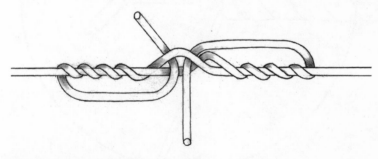

Chaytor knot, blood knot, barrel knot

Check-rein method
In fly tying, the check-rein method, devised by William Bayard Sturgis and illustrated in *Fly-Tying* (1940), erects dry-fly wings, especially quill wings. This method eliminates wing twist by using a thread "check-rein" loop to

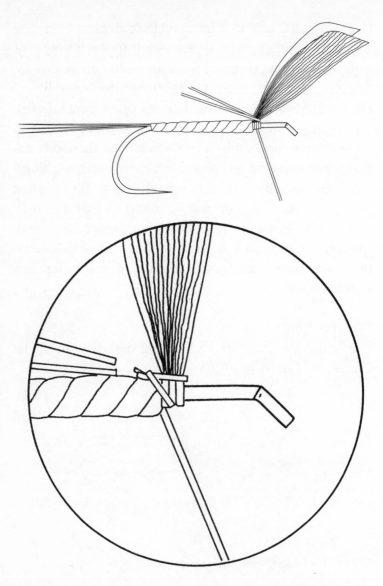

pull the wings back while the right thumb and index finger prevent the wing from buckling.

Chenille
The soft, tufted yarn with fibers that spiral from a central, twisted, two-strand core; from the French *chenille,* meaning caterpillar; a common and popular fly-tying material.

Chironomid

A nonbiting midge. There are more than 100 genera and 2,500 species in North America. The Chironomidae (Greek: *chironom, -us,* "one who moves the hands") take their name either from the plumose or palmated, handlike male antennae, or from "one who gestures with the hands," referring to the upraised waving forelegs of the adult. Anglers call the Chironomids *midges* or *gnats*; the Scottish, "blae and black;" and the English, "buzzers." The typical hooks for larvae, pupae, and adults range from size 16 to 26. The English term *buzzer* may describe its circular dance on the water surface before flight. See *Midge.*

Chironomid Larva Characteristics
1. Body length 1–20 mm (most 1–10 mm)
2. Body colors green, black, gray, yellow, tan, and red (the red species, sometimes termed *bloodworms,* contains hemoglobin)

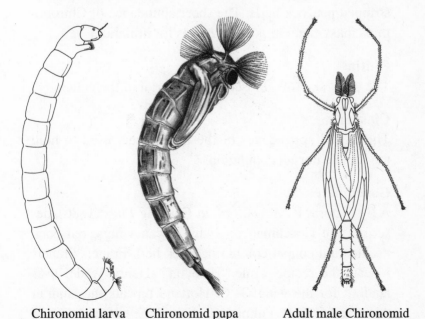

Chironomid larva   Chironomid pupa   Adult male Chironomid

3. Small, round head
4. No legs, but first thoracic and last abdominal segments have a pair of short, ventral prolegs
5. Many species live in slender silk tubes attached to the
   substrata of stream or lake

Chironomid Adult Characteristics
1. Body length 1–15 mm
2. Body color same range as larva
3. One pair of wings and one pair of minute balancing
   knobs or haltere (halters) in place of rear wings
4. Slender body and long, slender legs; front legs are the
   longest
5. Antennae with more than five segments, less than
   half of body length; males have bushy or hairy antennae (plumose antennae)

   In fly tying, the imitative elements include size, color,
slender body, and—for the adult—small, flat wings. The
distinctly segmented bodies are often imitated with
stripped peacock herls. The sheer abundance of Chironomids make them important insects for imitation.

Chitin
The outer skin of an insect; the material of the cuticle.

Claspers
The paired appendages of the male insect used to hold
the female during copulation.

Coachman
A fly pattern; F. M. Halford, in *Floating Flies* (1886), describes the Coachman fly: white swan wings, red cock
hackle, and copper-colored peacock herl. Francis Francis
repeats the recipe while "Halcyon" (Henry Wade) uses
landrail for the wing. T. C. Hofland repeats the landrail
wing, and G. P. R. Pulman substituted the white section of
a magpie wing-feather. David Foster's *Scientific Angler*

(sixth edition, undated) attributes the Coachman Fly to Tom Bosworth, the royal coachman to George IV, William IV, and Queen Victoria. "A favorite freak of his with the whip was to take the pipe from the teeth of a passing pedestrian by a carefully calculated whirl of the whip, and his aptitude was as remarkably exemplified, for a limited distance, in the use of the rod. Bosworth originated the Coachman Fly, so much appreciated for night-fishing." The Coachman pattern, both wet and dry, has many variations including the Royal Coachman (red center), the California Coachman (yellow center) and the Lead-wing Coachman (dark wing). Though after the fact, some attribute the red of the Royal Coachman to the red livery of the coachman.

Coch-y-bondhu
A furnace feather or cape with a black center and black listing or edge; from the Welsh, meaning red *(coch)* and black *(du* or *dhu)*; coch a bon dhu, meaning "red with black *(du)* trunk or stem *(pon)*"; an "angler's artificial fly," dated 1852 *(OED)*; the Welsh term for the terrestrial June bug *(Phylopertha horticola),* known also as the Brachen Clock, an insect that is red or reddish brown with a black belly; a term descriptive of such coloration; a pattern with red hackle or red wings and black body; several variant spellings including *cock y bondhu.* "A coch-y-bondhu hackle is one having a black center or list with red (reddish brown) or brown outer fibers tipped with black. This hackle is the same as the 'furnace' with the exception of the black outer edge" (Harold Smedley, *Fly Patterns and Their Origins* [1950]).

Collar
The gut leader. "We should always soak the gut previously to attempting to tie the links together, so as to make a collar" (H. C. Cutcliffe, *The Art of Trout Fishing on Rapid Streams* [1863]).

Complete metamorphosis
The physical changes in the development of an insect that include ovum, larva, pupa, and adult.

Compound eye
The insect eye, which composes numerous simple eyes functioning collectively. See also *Ocelli,* the simple eye.

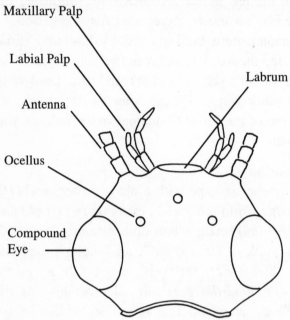

Maxillary Palp

Labial Palp

Antenna

Ocellus

Compound Eye

Labrum

Cop
"Some make the Body of the cop, or top Feather on the Head of a Plover or Lapwing" (James Chetham, *The Angler's Vade Mecum* [1700]). "A crest on the head of a bird, 1787" *(OED).*

Coq de Leon
The coq de Leon flock was originally bred in a Spanish monastery in about 1620. The coq de Leon feathers are "spade" feathers and not the traditional, dorsal-cervical hackle feather. They are stiff, glassy, and sometimes

finely flecked. Coq de Leon feathers are used for tails, legs, hackle, and wings. Two or three fibers make excellent mayfly tails. A small bundle creates a spinner's glassy wings, and a larger bundle imitates the mottled ambers and grays of a caddis wing.

The coq de Leon feathers may be divided into two groups: the browns *(pardos)*, and the grays *(indios)*. The mottled or speckled *pardos* are often highly desirable. Each group may then be subdivided into five browns *(corzuno, sarrioso, langareto, aconchado, flor de escoba)*, and five grays *(negrisco, acerado, plateado, rubion, palometa)*. Other variations of coq de Leon feathers are usually considered to be variations of these ten color types.

All of these feathers and various pattern types are described in *El Manuscrito de Astorga* (1624) by Juan de Bergara. The text has been translated into English by Claude Belloir and printed privately (1984) in Denmark by Preben Torp Jacobsen. The text includes a facsimile of the Old Spanish document and modern translations in Spanish, French, and English. Jesus Pariente Diez's *La Pesca de la Trucha en los rios de Leon* (1984) describes the patterns from the *Astorga* manuscript, by Luis Pena of Leon, dated 1825. The traditional Leon patterns, with or without tails, have thread ribbing, silk bodies, and hackles tied in a variety of color combinations. Some of the *Astorga* patterns, tied with wrapped hackles (turns of hackle), were used with a dapping rod: "This month March provides great sport for rod fishing because it is springtime and the zephyr and the *'favonio'* a pleasant breeze blow and the waters become warmer." The rod, much like the modern Spanish *tralla* or whip cracker, was used like a blow line or dapping rod.

The translucency of the coq de Leon barbs is made especially evident by rotating the feather in sunlight. The barbs appear to reflect all the gathered light until they burst into a particularly subtle and rich color. The glossy translucency and rigidity of the barbs make them excellent for patterns that require extremely fine barbs, approximately 0.002 of an inch, less than 15 millimeters long. Consequently, they make excellent tails for mayfly duns and spinners.

The *pardos* come from the Leon area and the *indios* from the extended highlands. For the modern tyer, the hackle fibers may be used as hackle barbs, tied according to the traditional Spanish patterns, or as tail fibers or spinner wings. There are various names for these Spanish feathers; however, most coq de Leon feathers may be classified according to five color categories within the brown and gray designation.

The term *pardo* is the name of a Spanish cock and means "reddish brown." The *Diccionario de la Real Academia,* quoted by Claude Belloir, defines the color as "the tint of earth or that of the fur of the common brown bear, intermediate between white and black, tinged with cinnamon, and darker than grey." Surely, this is where color surpasses description.

Pardo corzuno: The term comes from the Corzo, or European roebuck *(Capreolus capreolus)*. The feather has very fine mottled marks of pale russet brown flecking against a dark background. The feather markings are, in fact, darker than the roebuck's coat. Sometimes this feather is also described in terms of the coloration of the fallow deer.

Pardo sarrioso: The term comes from *sarrio,* a Spanish variety of the European wild goat or chamois *(Rupicapra rupicapra)*. This feather is similar to a finely mottled *corzuno,* but with a light brown background.

Pardo langareto: The original name was *longareto* from the Old Spanish *longo,* meaning long, with probable reference to a natural fly or to the rather large feather markings. On this feather, the markings are aligned or joined to form a pale (almost a pale Naples yellow) strip that appears as an inverted V.

Pardo aconchado: This feather gets its name from the color of the conch shell. The large markings on a light brown background are not aligned. In the commentary of the *Astorga* manuscript, *conchado* is defined as a "cock whose overall shade is speckled with another tint."

Pardo flor de escoba: This term comes from the coloration of the Spanish broom bush, genus *Genista.* The term *escoba* means broom. The dark background is nearly covered with reddish brown or pale burnt-umber spots or strips.

The coq de Leon *indio* feathers, a gray feather ranging from chalk white to a glossy black, are *indio negrisco* (gray black to black); *indio acerado* (steel gray or ash gray); *indio plateado* (silver gray or pearl gray); *indio avellanado* (hazelnut); *indio perla* (pearl); *indio rubion* (blond gray); and *indio palometa,* from *paloma,* meaning pigeon (gray-white to dusty white). The most interesting *indios* are the *negrisco,* the *acerado,* the *avellanado,* the *perla,* and the *rubion.*

Indio negrisco: The *indio negrisco* is a gray black to a deep lustrous black. The microscopic barbules of the webbing have a blue-green sheen similar to a peacock herl. The stem is a lustrous black.

Indio acerado: The *indio acerado* is a silver steel gray. The webbing is pale gray. The term *acerado* means steel and is also described as a silver ash-gray.

Indio avellanado: The *indio avellanado* is best described as a hazelnut color. It is a remarkable subtle blend of gray and brown that is apparent only in reflected light. The webbing is a light gray to a near white. The stem is usually gray.

Indio perla: The *indio perla* is, as the name suggests, a pearl color. It is similar to the *avellanado,* but slightly stronger in the metallic pearl sheen of the barbs.

Indio rubion: The barbs of the *indio rubion* are a bright ginger or a ruddy golden yellow. The webbing of this *indio* has, like the *indio negrisco,* the blue-green sheen of a peacock herl. *Rubion* is an Old Spanish term for red.

Coq de Leon spade feather: *Flor de Escoba*

Costa

The major, frontal forewing vein of an insect; the costal vein that forms the leading or anterior margin of an insect wing; the costal vein is one of the three nearly parallel longitudinal veins, which include the subcosta and radius.

Coxa

The basal or body segment of an insect leg; plural, *coxae*. See *Insect (nomenclature)*.

Cranefly

The family Tipulidae, the cranefly. Cranefly patterns appear early in tying history. Leonard West lists several imitations in *The Natural Trout Fly and Its Imitation* (1921). The cranefly is also called daddy-long-legs or harry-long-legs. See *Harry-long-legs*.

Cree

A tricolored feather with cream or pale ginger, red game, and black or gray; a hackle with black-and-red bars on a white ground; a mottled ginger; a cape of such coloration.

Creel

A feather or hackle with red bars on the white ground; sometimes called a ginger grizzly (i.e., a white feather with red bars rather than black bars), a ginger chinchilla, or barred red game; term is from a rare Old English game bird. The shortened name *cree* is also given to this bird; however, the cree feather should have both black and red bars on a white ground. See *Cuckoo*. Also a basket or container for fish.

Creeper

The stonefly nymph; any nymph or larva: "The creeper is the larva of the stonefly; it is called 'the devil's coach

horse' [and] is formidable looking but is quite harmless"
(G. W. Maunsell, *The Fisherman's Vade Mecum* [1952]).
See *Spinner.*

Crewel

"A thin worsted yarn" *(OED)*; a common, strand body
material used by early tyers.

Cubital intercalary veins

The paired, unconnected longitudinal veins occurring in
the insect wing. Note that the cubital region is the lower,
rear corner of the wing.

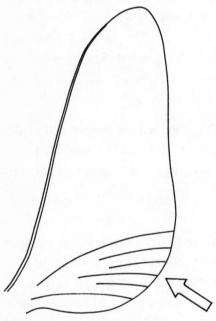

Cuckoo

Also *creel*; "mottled black and white" hackles. "Take a
cuckoo (Plymouth rock) hackle" (G. E. M. Skues, *Silk,
Fur and Feather* [1950]). George Leonard Herter, in *Professional Fly Tying, Spinning and Tackle Making* (1971),
concluded that "J. H. Hale calls grizzly hackle 'Cuckoo'
hackle, for what reason no one knows." Actually, the rea-

son is apparent: The male cuckoo's gray and white barred breast feathers suggest the similarly barred grizzly hackle. According to David Hawksworth's *British Poultry Standards* (1982), cuckoo barring is "Irregular barring where two colours are somewhat indistinct and run into each other, . . . as in the cuckoo leghorn and Marans." See *Grizzly.*

Cutaneous respiration
Cutaneous respiration occurs when an insect is able to breathe directly through the outer skin or cuticle. Such respiration is through the body wall itself.

Damselfly

The insect, suborder *zygoptera* (Greek *zygo* = yoke, hence "yoke-winged"). The gills of the damselfly nymph appear like three feathered paddles at the end of a slender abdomen. The nymph swims by body undulations, the gills functioning much like sculling oars. The nymph travels with minnowlike whipping motions. Most damselfly nymphs are a somewhat transparent pale yellow, tan, olive, or brown. Immediately before hatching (usually in June or July), the nymph migrates to shore in numbers. Such migrations during the morning hours will boil the water with slashing and rolling trout as they feed on the struggling nymphs. When at rest, the wings of the adult damselfly are folded parallel on top of the body with the edge up. The base width of the forewing and hind wing is nearly the same; the hind wings of the dragonfly are wider than the forewings.

Damselfly patterns, unlike dragonfly patterns, are a rather recent development. According to Marvin Nolte, damselfly patterns did not reach importance until after the late 1940s. In the 1950s, both William F. Blades and C. F. Walker tied adult damsel patterns.

Characteristics of the Damselfly Nymph
1. Three paddlelike tails (actually, caudal gill lamellae)
2. Large eyes
3. Modified and extendable capture lobes (the labia)

4. Long, slender body
5. Two pairs of wing pads
6. Whipping undulations of body when swimming
7. Inconspicuous bristlelike antennae

Characteristics of the Adult Damselfly
1. Four wings "yoked" or narrow at the base
2. When at rest, wings held together (often edge up and extended above and parallel to the body)
3. Large eyes, separated by more than their width

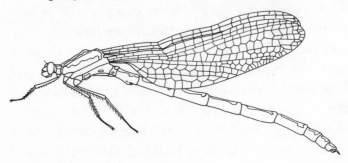

4. Inconspicuous bristlelike antennae
5. Unusual sexual organ (penis vesicle) on the ventral surface of the second abdominal segment

In fly tying, the imitative elements of nymph and adults include size, slender body, and colors. The brightly colored adults, with parallel wings, are often imitated.

Dapping

To fish with a light line (or silk blow line) with the line often attached directly to the end of the long rod (traditionally 12 to 18 feet), which allows the line to drift and dance in the wind as the fly gently touches the water; dapping, also dape or dib (*OED*, 1653). Dapping flies are usually fully dressed with stiff and heavy hackles on an extended hook. In this angling method, the natural insect or artificial fly is touched or danced on the water surface rather than cast. "To fish by letting the bait dip and bob lightly on the water" *(OED)*. Traditional loch (lake) dapping in Scotland and Ireland, where the boat drifts with a drogue, favored the large, palmered artificials or naturals, especially the mayfly, the daddy-long-legs, and the grasshopper. No reel was required, only a woven horsehair or silk blow-line. Also known as dibbing, shade-fishing, bushing, or bush-fishing (T. C. Hofland, *The British Angler's Manual* [1848]).

William Lawson (Lauson) edited the 1620 and later editions of John Dennys's *The Secrets of Angling*. Lawson's marginalia, which according to John Waller Hills included the "first mention of fly casting," described *bushing* or dapping: "If the winde be rough, and trouble the crust of the water, he will take it in the plaine deeps, and then, and there, commonly the greatest will rise. When you have hookt him, give him leave, keeping your line streight, and hold him from roots, and he will tire himselfe. This is the chiefe pleasure of angling. This flie and two linkes among wood, or close by a bush, moved in the crust of the water, is deadly in the evening, if you come close. This is called bushing for trouts." See *Blow line*.

This woodcut, from *A Handbook of Angling* (1848) by "Ephemera" [Edward Fitzgibbon], shows an angler in hiding dapping on leaves. Notice that the tapered rod lacks a reel. ". . . He drops his bait first on one of those leaves, and then by a sliding motion causes it to slip off, and fall on the water. The fish, taking this fall for a natural one, is not scared, but seizes the bait boldly."

Day fly

The mayfly; the Ephemeridae, sometimes casually rendered "lasting but a day," especially the larger drakes. Hooks for such were sold as day fly hooks. In England, the term mayfly, reserved for only a few Ephemeridae (*Ephemera danica, Ephemera vulgata,* and *Ephemera lineata),* is derived from the month of their appearance. Also called the Green Drake and Spent Gnat. See *Mayfly.*

Dee salmon fly

A salmon fly design characterized by (1) long, slender wings mounted low over the body; (2) long, straggling hackle, often originally heron; and (3) jungle cock mounted on the sides of the hackle rather than on the wing.

DeFeo style

Charles DeFeo mounted salmon and steelhead beards by clipping the V tip of a single feather, leaving an equal number of barbs on each side of the stem. The attached barbs are naturally apportioned and easily positioned. After mounting the feather beneath the shank, the feather is drawn forward to adjust the length and splay the barbs. The beard is then secured and the excess stem trimmed.

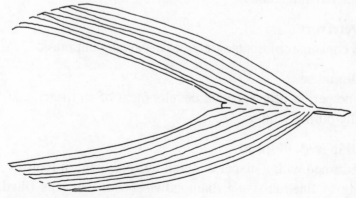

Clip the center to V the feather.

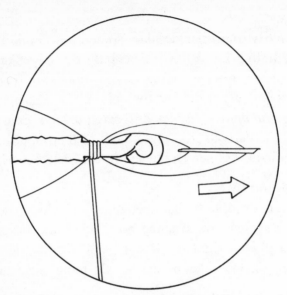

Mount the beard with the barbs beneath and the stem above the shank. Pull forward to adjust barb length, and secure with thread wraps. Trim excess.

Detached body
A term given to an artificial pattern with a body mounted *immediately* behind the wings. The body usually curves up and away (from the body or naked hook shank) in imitation of the adult mayfly, especially the large drakes. See *Extended body.*

Detrivore
A consumer of disintegrated or decayed plant mass.

Diapause
The period of suspended development of an insect, usually during winter.

Diapered, diapred
Adorned with a diaper or small uniform pattern (consisting of lines crossing diamondwise with the gaps filled with lines, dots, etc.) such as found on diapered linen

(OED). "To diversify the surface, to variegate" *(OED)*. "Camlet fly. Is taken from the middle of May, until the end of June, is in shape like a Moth, with fine Diapred or water Wings, and make of a dark-brown shining Camlet, rib'd over with very small light green Silk . . ." (James Chetham, *The Angler's Vade Mecum* [1700]). "Water-wings" are those fine, transparent wings without pattern or markings.

Dinging
To mount the tying thread to the bare hook. ". . . My first step is to pick up the hook and start the dinging with a piece of thread long enough to tie the fly" (Lee Wulff, "The Wulff Fly Patterns," *Roundtable,* January/February, 1979). Perhaps from the implication of "to knock," "to hit upon," "to strike" *(OED)*. Ding, with a variant dent, "to strike or hurl" (Eric Partridge, *Origins* [1983]).

Distal
The outermost apex of a structure; the part farthest from the body; opposed to basal or proximal; said of insect parts.

Diurnal
Occurring in daytime; adapted for daytime or daylight; opposed to nocturnal.

Dorsal
The top or back side of an organism.

Doubled hackle
Folding hackle barbs together on one side of the hackle. The singular advantage to a folded hackle—as opposed to a single-sided, stripped hackle—is that the hackle has twice the number of barbs per stem length. The singular disadvantage is that the barbs, unless remarkably soft, may skew awry.

J. H. Hale, in *How to Tie Salmon Flies* (1930), notes that the underside of the hackle should be uppermost. T. E. Pryce-Tannatt, in *How to Dress Salmon Flies,* writes that the good side of the feather, the bright side, should be uppermost. George Kelson, in *The Salmon Fly: How to Dress It and How to Use It* (1895), describes the process in detail. "The bright side being downwards, pull the stalk of the hackle in pliers straight and not at an angle across. Then take the point between finger and thumb of the left hand, let the pliers hang loose in the palm of the right with the hackle lying on your first finger and joint bright side downwards. By lowering the point held in the left finger and thumb downwards, *strain* the hackle stalk so that the fibres tend to stand upwards toward you."

Dragonfly
The insect, suborder anisoptera (from Greek *anis* = unequal, hence "unequal wings"). The adult dragonfly holds its wings at right angles to the body while in flight or repose. The nymphs appear in still or slow waters and, although not as abundant as insects such as the mayfly, can attain a length of more than 30 millimeters before emergence. Their size alone is enough to support large trout. The order Odonata, which the dragonfly shares with the delicate damselfly, refers to the toothed labium or "lower lip" that extends nearly one-third the body length and functions as a capture lobe. They are predaceous in their nymphal stages, particularly in the stages near emergence (the senior instars), and devour nymphs, larvae, and even small fish. Leonard West, in *The Natural Trout Fly and Its Imitation* (1921), calls the dragonfly nymph the *bête noire* of caddis larvae: "The long spear with which they are armed, proving a capital weapon for poking the Caddis-worm out of the protecting sheath."

When ready for transformation to the adult stage, the nymph usually crawls out of the water onto rocks or plant stems for the final molt. Once out of the final nymphal husk, the newly hatched (teneral) adult is soft and a pale yellow for some hours or days. The adult will expand its wings to full size in about a half hour. Male and female adults are usually similar in color, although the male may be brighter.

Characteristics of the Dragonfly Nymph
1. Large compound eyes
2. Inconspicuous bristlelike antennae
3. Extendable labium
4. Internal rectal gills
5. Usually a compact, corpulent body, often oval or triangular in cross section

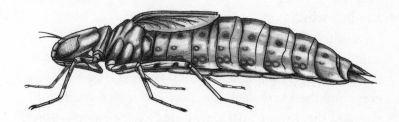

6. Locomotion by rectal expulsion of water
7. Six clustered legs moved forward on the thorax
8. Modified and extendable capture lobes (the labium)

Characteristics of the Adult Dragonfly
1. Large compound eyes
2. Inconspicuous bristlelike antennae
3. No tail
4. Two pairs of large wings held horizontally, often tilted up or down, when at rest
5. Eyes never separated by more than their own width
6. Superb fliers that capture insects with their "net" legs during flight
7. Unusual sexual organ (penis vesicle) on the ventral surface of the second abdominal segment

Movement is the result of the rapid expelling of water from their anal cavity that functions as a rectal gill because of the thin-walled lower intestine. This anal respiration produces an unusual swimming pattern. The common expulsive attitude consists of a slightly arched body with the legs relaxed and folded beneath the thorax. The abdomen dilates and contracts both in length and diameter during propulsion. The movement is a fast-slow sequence, and the nymphs sink momentarily before another expulsion of water propels them up and forward. They seldom travel long distances through open water; they live a furtive existence among the plants and debris. The length of the explosive glide depends on speciation and maturation of the nymphs. The dragonfly nymph averages 22 millimeters in length and 7 millimeters in abdominal width.

For the fly fisher, the dragonfly nymphs may be classified according to two habitat types: the plant clingers (such as the *Aeshnidae*), which actively pursue their prey, and the burrowers or silters (such as the *Libellulidae* and the western riffle-dwelling *Gomphidae*), which either camouflage themselves with silt and algae or burrow into the marl and mud. The more predaceous clingers usually have an ovoid cross section. There are, naturally, distinctions between the burrowers and silters, but for practical purposes, both may be considered bottom dwellers. The silters have minute hairs or horns that assist in camouflage, whereas the burrowers have somewhat flattened or shovel-shaped body parts for digging. The burrowers and silters normally strike only when their prey is within labium range. Both the burrowers and clingers inhabit the marginal epilimnion of the lake. Their general coloration tends toward the mottled deep olives, bright greens, and dark browns, with often intricate, cryptic stippling and delicate runic etchings along the abdominal plates. The nymphs that conceal themselves in the silt and mud appear, for the most part, dull and mottled, whereas the olive and brown nymphs usually inhabit the plant mats.

Charles Bowlker's *The Art of Angling* (1839) lists the first specific dragonfly patterns *(Libella or Libellula)*: "The wings are made of a reddish brown feather from the wing of a cock turkey, the body of auburn-coloured mohair wrapped with yellow silk, and a ginger cock's hackle wrapped under the wing; the hook No. 2 or 3. Or it may be varied thus; the wings of a rich brown feather from a heron's wing; the body drab, or olive-coloured mohair, a bittern's hackle under the wings, and a forked tail. This fly is about two inches in length."

Conrad Voss Bark, in *A History of Flyfishing* (1992), asserts that the large, winged salmon patterns, usurping the "Roman plumes," imitated the large dragons and damsels, "giving them several pairs of wings and a rather thick dubbed body for the dragonfly, a thinner body, probably bright blue, for the damsel fly." Although scientifically unsound, salmon fly patterns may have originally imitated the larger insects—dragonflies, moths, and, as once claimed, butterflies.

In fly tying, the imitative elements of the dragonfly nymph include size, spindle shape, and mottled color. Size, shape, and *retrieve* are probably the essential imitative elements. Adult patterns with stiff, extended wings usually defy casting; soft, collapsible wings are usually preferred.

Drake

Any member of a number of specific, large mayflies, such as the Brown Drake *(Ephemera simulans)* and Green Drake *(Ephemera guttulata, Ephemerella grandis,* etc.). The term *drake* is also used for any mayfly, or

Ephemeroptera, regardless of size (Michael Theakson and Louis Rhead). Perhaps the term is related to or derived from Old English *draca,* meaning dragon (compare dragonfly and drake); or the male duck (Old English *duce,* to dive). The term appears to describe any large flier and first appeared as an angling term in the *Treatyse* (1496). According to Harold Hinsdill Smedley in *Fly Patterns and Their Origins* (1950), the term *drake* was first applied to mayflies because their wings could be imitated with feathers from the mallard drake; Smedley also quotes the line, "A dun is a half done drake," with the implication that a drake is a sexually mature mayfly.

The term *drake* has an interesting tying history. A "drake flye" appears as early as *The Treatyse of Fysshynge Wyth an Angle* (1496). It had a "body of blacke wull & lappyd abowte wyth blacke sylke" with the "wynges of the mayle of the blacke drake wyth a blacke heed." John Waller Hills, in *A History of Fly Fishing for Trout* (1971), reads "mayle of the blacke drake wyth a blacke heed" as either "some dark mallard feather" from a black-headed drake (?) or as a specific dark-based feather. Nineteenth-century mayfly patterns often utilized whole drake body feathers for mayfly wings. Perhaps for obvious tying reasons, these large mayfly patterns came to be called drakes. Leonard West, in *The Natural Trout Fly and Its Imitation* (1921), lists nine different tying styles—including "An upright, whole-feather winged fly as a Drake."

Thus the term *drake* became generic for any large pattern—including large mayflies like the brown drake, green drake, and yellow drake—tied with a whole drake body feather. Describing the green drake pattern, Charles Cotton, in *The Complete Angler* (Part Two), offers a novel and, presumably, "questionless" derivation of the term *drake*: "His body is, in some, of a paler, in others, of a darker yellow; for they are not all exactly of a colour, ribbed with rows of green, long, slender, and growing sharp towards the tail, at the end of which he has three long small whisks of a very dark colour, almost black, and his tail turns up towards his back like a Mallard; from whence, questionless, he has the name of Green Drake." James Chetham, in *The Angler's Vade Mecum* (1700), also continues the analogy: he notes that the tail of the Green Drake "turns up towards his Back, like a Mallard, from whence he has his name of Greendrake." The tipped or cocked tail appears on some early drake patterns.

Draper hook

A hook bend characterized by a double shank brazed at the bend to produce a "flat-bodied" nymph hook. The concept, originated by Keith Draper of New Zealand, was refined and produced by Partridge & Sons in 1980. The "shoulders" of the hook body have fine serrations to prevent material movement.

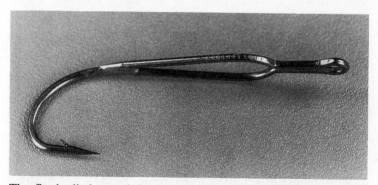

The flat-bodied nymph hook, developed by Keith Draper of New Zealand in 1977, features a wide gap, short spear, and point. The looped shank, bronzed at the bend, forms the hook eye. Note the shoulder serrations that help secure body materials.

Dressing
(1) The material, such as furs or feathers, or (2) the process of mounting the material on the hook; the recipe, which may include methods as well as materials, used in tying a specific artificial fly pattern.

Drogue
A drift or water anchor usually made of canvas about 3 or 4 feet square that slows the natural drift of a boat. The drogue, a term of unknown origin, was used to check the speed of a whale (1725), and was a hooped canvas bag towed at the stern of a boat to prevent broaching (until 1875) *(OED)*. Drogues may have a painter or tripping line and an attached float, such as cork, to control drift depth and "to keep the anchor from sinking" (W. S. Jackson, *Notes of a Fly Fisher* [1933]).

Dropper(s)
One or more of the artificial flies mounted above the tail or point fly on a leader. See also *Stretcher.*

Dry fly
An artificial fly that floats on the surface of the water. The traditional requirements for a dry fly are (1) an imitation of the winged stage of an adult insect (subimago or imago); (2) a presentation, usually to an individual trout or trout rise; (3) a natural float or drift of an imitation; (4) the drying of the imitation during the backcast; (5) a pattern pulled or "skated" across the water surface.

The factors that determine whether an artificial fly floats or sinks include (1) hook weight, (2) hackle quantity, (3) hackle quality, (4) hackle stance, (5) applied dressing, (6) pattern design, (7) pattern materials, (8) casting action, (9) surface area, and (10) tail design.

The authoritative definition of the dry fly comes from Vincent Marinaro's *In the Ring of the Rise* (1976). "We must begin with the proposition that no matter how dry the fly is, it must touch the water and be exposed to the air at the same time. If this idea is carried out to its logical conclusion, all must agree that if the smallest portion is exposed to the air no matter how deeply submerged the fly may be, it is still a legitimate form of the dry fly." Thus, low-floating emergers and swamped spinners are "dry" when they touch air. In short, Marinaro conceded that "any fly, natural or artificial, touching the surface film, whether it be on the film, in the film, or mostly under the film" is a dry fly.

John Waller Hills dates the 1851 edition of G. P. R. Pulman's *The Vade Mecum of Fly-Fishing for Trout* as the first published observations on the dry fly. He also adds that dry-fly fishing was probably practiced on the river Itchen in England during the 1840s. By 1865, the practice of the dry fly was prevalent on the southern Hampshire streams in England. In *Ogden on Fly Tying* (1887), James Ogden establishes 1839 as the date that he invented the dry fly. "Some forty years ago, when I introduced my floating flies. . . ."

The modern dry fly may include patterns that "swim" in the surface—such as the so-called flymphs (see *flymph*), "damp" patterns, emergers, and parachute patterns—as well as patterns that penetrate the water surface with the body or hook, such as the Swisher-Richards no-hackle patterns. A dry fly may be any pattern that is visible above the water surface, hence any pattern that extends above the water surface. Thus, a spinner may be considered a dry pattern. The distinction between the dry fly and the wet fly is not as clear as it was during the last century. A "wet" fly may include the traditional wet fly as well as any pattern that is entirely submerged. With the advent of fishing the various stages of a particular insect, fly patterns and fly hooks have become more specific.

Some patterns, in fact, may be fished as dry, emerger, and wet in a single cast or drift. At the end of a dry float, the pattern may be tugged beneath the surface to imitate a sunken nymph and then, on the retrieve, pulled close to the surface to imitate an emerger. Thus, the manner of presentation and line technique may define or determine the pattern type.

A few "flutter" patterns are technically dry; though they are "damp" or "moist" when scraped along the water surface. Usually, nymphs or larvae are specialized wet patterns, and floating emergers are dry patterns. Generically, any patterns without a completely submerged hook may be considered a dry fly. A completely submerged or saturated dry fly is a wet fly; a dry fly fished as a wet fly is a wet fly.

With numerous and notable exceptions, a dry fly *may* be:
1. Any pattern with a rigid or supporting tail and hackle that elevates a portion of the hook above the water surface
2. Any pattern that incorporates an effective amount of nonabsorbent materials, or any pattern that has a flotant added before presentation
3. Any pattern proportioned and tied so that the hook does not completely penetrate the water surface
4. Any pattern tied in such a manner that the natural tips touch but do not completely penetrate the water surface, i.e., any pattern based on the principle of hydrofuge
5. Any pattern tied in such a manner that the dull or concave side of the stiff hackle faces the hook eye
6. Any pattern with vertical, forward, or horizontal wings
7. Any pattern that occupies three dimensions, i.e., any pattern hackled so that the barbs radiate at right angles from the hook-shank axis

8. Any pattern tied on a light-wire hook (such as a forged sneck, sproat, or perfect) with nonabsorbent materials or materials dressed so that the pattern floats on or in the surface film

Dub

"To dress a fly, or a hook and line with fly" 1450 *(OED)*. The earliest meaning is to dress or adorn, thus it came to mean to cover or wrap material on a hook. Like the term *arm,* dub may also refer to the act of attaching a fly to a line. The term *dub fly* sometimes indicated any artificial fly, in contrast to the natural insect used as bait. "And herein I find no small difficulty by written directions, perfectly . . . to teach any . . . how to make an Artificial, or Dub-fly" (James Chetham, *The Angler's Vade Mecum* [1700]).

Dubbing

Currently, any natural or synthetic fibers wrapped on a hook; the application or technique for applying such fibers; the twisting of fibers on a thread or thread loop to form a chenille-like strand.

It is impossible to say when dubbing—mounting fur or hair on a thread, which is then wrapped forward along the hook shank—first appeared. We know more about winging and hackling than dubbing. As far back as 1450, dubbing meant to dress, to array, to adorn, or to invest, apparently in any manner, including "dubbing" a knight. The term *dubbing* refers to any manner of "dressing" a hook, whether wrapping a body or attaching a line. Most early tying descriptions suggest that the body material was a short skein tied in at the bend and then wrapped forward rather than spun on a thread. In the second century, Marcus Valerius Martialis, or Martial, writes of "fraudful flies," but does so without description. "Crimson wool" wrapped around a hook took "spotted fish," according to Aelianus's *De Natura Animalium,* but this early third-century work does not tell us how the hook was wrapped. And the *Treatyse* (1496) describes a "body of blacke wull & lappid abowte wt yelow threde" without detail. The *Astorga* manuscript (1624) by Juan de Bergara refers to the color of hare and camel fur, but the bodies are, apparently, strands of silk, linen, or "sieve canvas." John Donne, a seventeenth-century poet, sings of the "curious traitors, sleeve-silk flies" ("The Baite," 1633). According to John Waller Hills, Thomas Barker, in the middle of the seventeenth century, gives us the first detailed tying instructions, which again are indeterminate: Wrap in the body and ribbing, make the body, and overrun the tinsel.

But by the eighteenth century (and very likely much earlier), we encounter current dubbing techniques. In Izaak Walton's *The Complete Angler* (the later Hawkins edition of 1766), an extended footnote lists important dubbing materials: bear, camel, badger, camlet (see *Camlet*), turkey carpet yarn, seal fur, hog's wool, squirrel tail, fox, otter, yellow fur of the marten, hare, and foumart (polecat), and barge-sail "under which there is almost a continual smoak [*sic*] arising from the fire and steam of the beef kettle," which in time "dyes the tilt [awning made from discarded wool sails] of a fine brown." The short furs—such as the marten's fur that came "from off the gills or spots under the jaws"—must have required mounting directly to the thread. Although there are other examples to plump the tale of dubbing, the truth must be nigh to 1700. Ted Niemeyer, fly-tying historian, believes that dubbing methods, as we understand them, date about 1750 or earlier. He bases his verdict on an antique pattern, resplendent with fiery-brown pig's wool dubbing. We may never know when a tyer first discovered that crewel, silk, or fur—perhaps too short to be applied directly on a hook—could be mounted to the thread and then wound along the shank.

Dubbing block

See *Spinning block.*

Dubbing brush

Fur or hair spun tightly between two *wire* strands. An electric dubber (for making dubbing brushes) was introduced in 1986 at a meeting of Czechoslovakian fly fishermen in České Budějovice. To make a dubbing brush, the spinner should produce dense twists, eighteen or more per centimeter, to lock in each hair or fiber. Dubbing brushes, which are available in various natural and synthetic fibers, are commonly used for body materials.

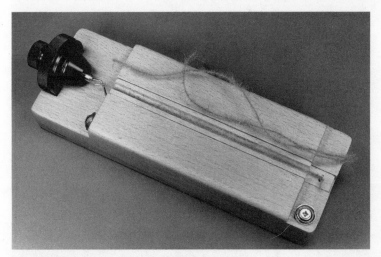

Modern Czech spinner and dubbing brushes

Dubbing comb

A fly-tying tool that extracts the vellus or underfur from fur and hair. Fly-tying historian Marvin Nolte finds the first reference to the dubbing comb for extracting underfur in G. P. R. Pulman's *The Vade Mecum of Fly-Fishing for Trout* (1851): "Body, blue fur from a hare or squirrel's

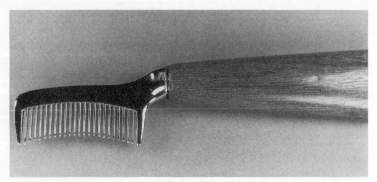

Modern Matarelli dubbing comb

skin (found among the roots and collected with a small-tooth comb)." Unlike the dubbing rake, which cuts hairs, this small, fine-toothed comb made by Frank Matarelli extracts the vellus—the short, soft "down" hairs—from fur or hair already cut from the hide. See *Dubbing rake.*

Dubbing loop

In fly tying, a loop, usually a thread loop, that traps and holds dubbing when spun. The technique was illustrated

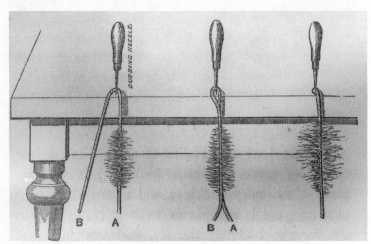

Halford dubbing loop method

and popularized in Frederic M. Halford's *Floating Flies and How to Dress Them* (1886). Halford looped thread over a dubbing needle stuck in the table edge. After applying dubbing to one strand, both strands were tightly spun to trap the dubbing. Halford used the method to create fur "hackles." "The effect of this will be to twist up the silk and fur between the two ends of it . . . into a rough-looking hackle, which is used exactly like an ordinary one, the silk representing the central quill and the fur the fibres of the hackle." Halford also recommends using the dubbing loop to create true hackles by inserting feather barbs in the dubbing loop.

Dubbing-loop lock
A tying thread maneuver that consolidates the two strands of a dubbing loop at the hook shank. The wrap creates a single spinning point with minimal bulk.

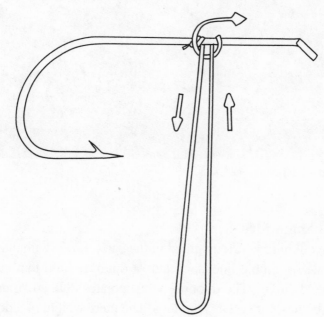

Dubbing-loop lock

Dubbing rake

A fly-tying tool, sometimes called the Belgium dubbing
rake, which, when stroked in the direction of fur growth
on animal hides, significantly separates the underfur
from the guard hairs. The guard hairs may be then
plucked from the dubbing. Furthermore, it slashes the fur
to various lengths, facilitating dubbing. The toothed cutter, made from steel or ceramics, usually has sharp and
beveled inside edges that shear and scrape. With light
strokes, the beveled cutters remove the underfur with
minimal guard hairs. With heavy strokes, the dubbing
rake crops the guard hairs as well.

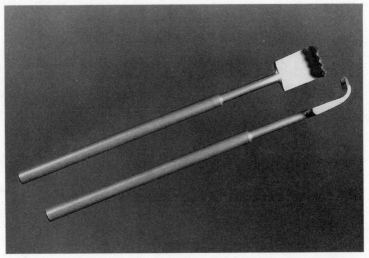

Modern dubbing rake

Dubbing whirl

The dubbing whirl, invented in the early 1980s with either
single or double hooks, creates a dubbing loop that cap-
tures dubbing. The dubbing whirl creates dubbed strands
for bodies, fur collars, and legs. The mere weight of a double-hook whirl, when "on the dangle," closes the pliant
hooks, thereby trapping any material placed within the

loop. Short strips of various furs, with a hide line attached, are placed in the dubbing loop. The hide line is then trimmed, leaving the fibers trapped in the loop. The whirl is then spun tightly to create a fur brush. Marabou barbs and sparse deer hair may also be spun in this manner. To create a fine microdubbing, hang the whirl on the loop. Wax and apply diced mole dubbing to one strand only. When spun, the dubbing, mounted on a single thread, creates a fine haze around the twisted, double threads.

Single thread method: Hang the thread from the hook bend and apply a soft, high-tack wax. Then distribute the dubbing evenly on the thread. Hang the dubbing whirl at the bottom of the dubbed strand and then fold the thread back to the hook bend, thereby creating a dubbing loop. Secure the thread with several wraps and spiral the thread forward. Only one thread of the dubbing loop will have dubbing. Tightly spin the dubbing whirl and wrap the dubbed body forward.

Double thread method: Mount the thread and make an appropriate-length dubbing loop. Wrap the working thread around the loop base at the shank. (See *Dubbing-loop lock.*) This gathers the loop and allows it to twirl from a single point. Then spiral the thread forward to the tie-off point. Attach the whirl hook or hooks to the bottom of the loop. Notice that by pulling down on the whirl, the double hooks come together to capture any material within the loop. Place the appropriate amount of dubbing within the spinning loop and push this dubbing "sliver" to the shank. Pull down on the whirl to trap the dubbing. Then, while keeping the loop closed to trap the dubbing, drape the end of the dubbing loop over the left index finger and spin the whirl with a clockwise motion (as viewed from above). By slowly moving the thread back and forth across the left index finger, the spin is transferred to the dubbing loop. Once tightly spun, the

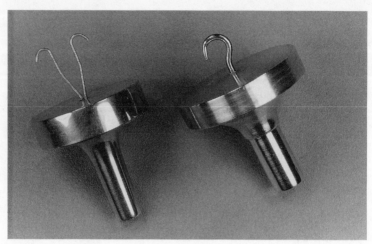

Double and single-hook dubbing whirls

dubbing loop may then be wrapped forward to create the body. Faux hackles may also be created in this manner.

An efficient dubbing whirl has several features, including (1) adequate weight and design for stable spinning, (2) thread hooks that will not slip, (3) double-hook whirls that close the spinning loop by its weight or a light pull, (4) single-hook models that have a stable spin on the central axis, (5) size small enough to hang beneath the vise jaws, and (6) a secure hold on the dubbing loop when wrapping the body.

Dun

(1) The sexually immature adult mayfly, the subimago; (2) the gray color of the subimago wing; the color iron-gray or grayish-brown derived from the Old English term *dunn*. The *Treatyse* (1496), where the angling term first appeared, included two March Duns and the Dun Cut.

Ecdysis

The act of casting or shedding the integument or outer skin; molting, to shed the exoskeleton; said of insects.

Eclosion

The act of hatching from the egg or from the pupal stage; the hatching into the adult stage; said of insects. Note that the term eclosion is equivalent to the angling term *hatch.*

Elytron

The platelike forewing of beetles that covers the membranous underwing; the anterior, chitinous wings of a beetle (*elytra,* plural).

Engine

Walton's engine. A small hand-crank tool for making horsehair fly lines, as depicted in *The Complete Angler:* "... I would recommend an engine lately invented, which is now to be had at almost any Fishing-tackle shop in London; it consists of a large horizontal wheel and

Antique Engine in the Ian Hay Collection—the hooks spin the same direction when furling and forming the horsehair links.

three very small ones, inclosed [*sic*] in a brass box about a quarter of an inch thick, and two inches in diameter; the axis of each of the small wheels is continued through the under-side of the box, and is formed into a hook: by means of a strong screw it may be fixed to any post or partition, and is set in motion by a small winch in the centre of the box" (Izaak Walton, *The Complete Angler* [1766]). The engine produced a three-strand twisted (or furled) horsehair line section.

To prevent the hooks from breaking the horsehair, a short length of wool yarn attaches between the hooks and the hairs. Cranking the handle spins the strands, thus forming the links. When taken off the winder, the three spun strands furl together to make a line section. Each line section is made with a decreasing number of strands that, when tied together, create a tapered horsehair fly line. When completed, the total fly line, according to *The Complete Angler* (1766), "must be 'very strong' and should be about eighteen or twenty [horse] hairs at the

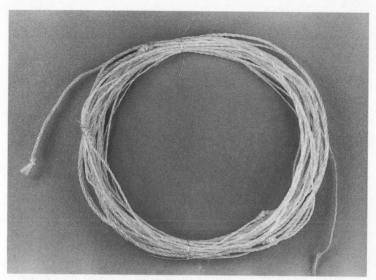

A traditional, twisted (furled) horsehair fly line made in Italy. Note the line taper and water knots that connect the links.

top, and so diminishing insensibly [imperceptibly] to the hook." Richard Niven, in *The British Angler's Lexicon* (1892), praised the tool: "Twisting Engine is a useful little appliance for twisting gut and hair into snoods, and may be had at any respectable tackle shop."

Salmon reel and horsehair fly line, ca. 1900.

Entry

An artificial fly has "good entry" when it creates little or no disturbance upon entering the water. "A wet fly which swims naturally and smoothly when drawn through the water is said to have good entry" (G. W. Maunsell, *The Fisherman's Vade Mecum* [1952]). A wet trout fly "ought to be so constructed as to swim with the smoothness of a nymph or small fish, and not to skirt or to carry bubbles. The commonest cause of such a defect in an artificial fly is too big and clumsy a head. This is the reason why an artificial wet fly usually has a head much smaller in proportion than that of the natural fly" (G. E. M. Skues, *The Way of a Trout with a Fly* [1935]). Skues also noted that "a small head alone will not ensure a good entry for a winged fly or for a fly with stiff hackles." He argued that eyed hooks are not as suitable for small trout flies as blind hooks because "the eye and the knot combine to make a disproportionately bulky head," thus inducing a poor entry.

Epilimnion

The upper water layer of a lake in summer. During summer, lake waters become stratified (thermal stratification) into two basic layers: a warmer upper layer and a colder lower layer. The lower layer is the hypolimnion. The narrow band between the two layers, where the temperature rapidly changes from one layer to the next, is the thermocline. Wind constantly circulates and mixes the water of the epilimnion. The hypolimnion, isolated by the thermocline, essentially maintains an approximate constant temperature. The depth of the epilimnion is dependent on wind force and light penetration. In fall, when the surface (the epilimnion) cools to the same temperature as the lower layer (the hypolimnion), then, because of matching water densities and autumn winds, the lake becomes unstratified. In shallow lakes, winter ice may completely cover the surface, thus preventing plants from removing carbon dioxide from the water. Fish mortality that is due to this condition is termed *winter kill*. In the shallow hypolimnion of small lakes or ponds, where waste products of decomposition build up, creatures may asphyxiate. When a number of fish perish in this manner, it is termed *summer kill*.

Expressionism
See *Imitation.*

Extended body
An extended, artificial-fly body that projects beyond or above the hook shank. Extended bodies have been tied for more than 100 years. Early tyers called extended bodies either detached (when mounted immediately behind the wings) or semidetached (when mounted at midshank or farther aft). The earliest illustration of an extended body, the detached Winged Larva, appears in William Blacker's *The Art of Fly-Making* (1855). Blacker used "the shrivelled larva" (the vacuous silk capsule) attached to the end of salmon gut. There are special hooks, such as Partridge K10 Yorkshire Fly Body Hook (a 1991 improved design first patented by Peter Mackenzie-Philps in 1973), with a wire extension for the body. The Yorkshire hook has nearly double the weight of an ordinary dry-fly hook. The extension, however, permits rapid tying, and the design hides the hook point in the hackle. Extended bodies appear primarily on mayfly drakes, damsel nymphs, and adult dragonflies. Although often rejected for their stiff, unnatural bodies, extended bodies may be soft and supple. Some extended-body patterns effectively conceal the hook point in heavy hackle. Most major angling writers have presented patterns for extended bodies. The following elements create an effec-

The extended-body, fan-winged mayfly in *A Quaint Treatise on Flees, and the Art of Artyfichall Flee Making,* (London, 1876. [The John Head Collection]). Aldam's *A Quaint Treatise* includes actual flies and fly-tying materials. John Waller Hills believed that the two mounted mayflies in *A Quaint Treatise,* including this one, are "the oldest representations of floating flies now extant." Both mayflies are attributed to James Ogden, the author of *Ogden on Fly Tying* (1887). Note the unusual *vertical-eyed* hook. See also David Foster's *The Scientific Angler* (undated), plate VI, figure 4, where a hook-eye "loop projects upwards."

tive extended body. The body should (1) be soft and supple; (2) arch away from the bend or shank; (3) be durable; (4) match the diameter, length, and shape of the natural; (5) never wrap around the hook bend; (6) never hinder the take; and (7) be quickly constructed from common materials. See *Yorkshire Flybody hook.*

Exuvia
The insect "shuck"; the cast cuticle or outer skin during molting; the vacant exoskeleton cast off after molting.

Fan wings

Dry-fly wings formed by two small, somewhat circular breast feathers, often from a wood duck or mallard drake, mounted to curve outward.

Feather (nomenclature)

The flat part of the feather, usually called the *vane,* is supported by the rachis. The *rachis* is that section of the shaft that bears the barbs. Unlike the quill (or calamus), the rachis is essentially solid instead of tubular. The vane is held together by parts called barb, barbule, and hooklet. *Barbs* branch out from the rachis in a single plane. The barbs, sometimes mistakenly called barbules, are the common fiber strips of the feather. The *barbules,* several hundred on each barb, interlock with nearby *hooklets* to hold the vane together. Barbs may bear barbules, which in turn may also bear barbicels. These barbicels commonly end in hooked hamuli that interlock with adjacent barbs, creating a continuous vane. The barbs act as natural zippers, locking the vane together. When preening, a bird zips the barbs together with its beak to reform the feather. What the tyer calls *webbing* is nothing more than the mat of dense barbules. These dense barbules trap moisture and increase the weight of the fly—characteristics not preferred in a dry fly.

The *calamus* is the barbless, tubular base of the rachis or shaft, which grows from the skin follicle. The *rachis* is the stiff, solid quill-like stem that extends from the calamus and that carries the barbs. The *barbs* (rami) are the hackle fibers that extend from the opposite side of the rachis or stem. The *barbules* are minute structures that extend from the barbs, creating a webby mat. The *flue* or *fluff* is the downlike fibers near the stem base. The *aftershaft* or *hyporachis* should be restricted to the auxiliary shaft only. The aftershaft has also been called the accessory plume—a hypoptile. The *afterfeather,* the soft accessory plume, varies in type—in grouse, quail, and pheasant, the afterfeather is long and narrow with relatively short barbs; in turkey, the afterfeather is often oval or elliptical with long, fine barbs that are one-third to two-thirds the length of the main vane; in ducks, the afterfeather is very short with no central stem or hyporachis.

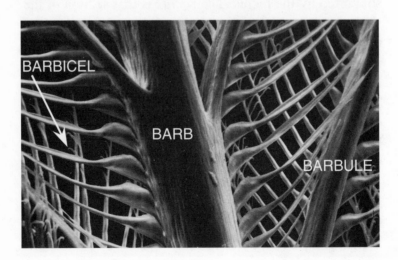

Feather orientation

There are two opposite feather orientations: the *Pryce-Tannatt* and the *zoological*. T. E. Pryce-Tannatt, in *How to Dress Salmon Flies* (1914) defines feather orientation: "If you take the centre tail feather of any bird . . . and hold it in front of you for examination by the stem with the tip pointing upwards and the 'best' side towards you . . . you would regard the fibres to the right as being 'right side' fibres, and those to the left as 'left side' fibres. Although, zoologically speaking, I believe this is incorrect, nevertheless for fly-dressing purposes it is most convenient. . . ." In contrast, the zoological orientation considers the feather an organism with its own left and right sides. Thus, if an eyed or ocellated peacock tail feather is positioned "face" or best side toward me, then the *right* side of the feather is on my *left* side as I view the feather. When a tyer refers to the left or right side of a feather, feather orientation should be understood.

Femur

The third leg segment of an insect, numbering from the body axis outward, which is usually broad. See *Insect (nomenclature)*.

Filiform

Threadlike or hairlike.

Filoplume

A hairlike feather; the mature filoplume has a threadlike shaft with a tuft of short basal barbs or barbules. Unlike a bristle, the filoplume has a tuft of barbs (the apical barbs) at the tip; it is a degenerate feather bearing apical barbs. There are usually two or three filoplumes with each body contour feather or semiplume, and they are more numerous near the remiges and rectrices.

Fitchew

Also *foumart:* "The fur of the polecat" *(OED).* "The [fly] tail of three hairs from a ... fitchew's tail" (Charles Bowlker, *The Art of Angling* [1839]).

Flat bend

Even early hooks reveal remarkable designs. W. Guise & Sons Limited of Redditch created a flat bend for tender-mouthed game fish such as grayling. The broad bend supposedly captured more tissue and increases hook strength.

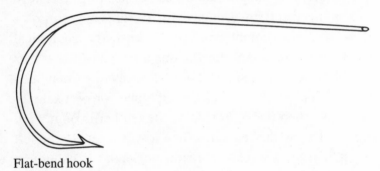

Flat-bend hook

Flax

Various shades of animal fur, especially wild hare fur; any soft, pale straw-colored fur or hair. "Now first catch your hare, and let this one be an old Jack hare, at the end of the season. . . . March hare if you can find one insane enough to be caught; brush or stroke his flax down very carefully over the back, and make it quite smooth, and then take a very sharp razor and shave him downwards, only over the back. . . . Shave an old doe and a leveret, the younger the better; and you will find the younger flax more fawn colour, and not black or red; whilst the older flax is darker, interspersed with some blackish hairs, and has a red or rusty shade as it were throughout it. . . ." (H. C. Cutcliffe, *The Art of Trout Fishing on Rapid Streams* [1863]). See *Hare's flax* and *Leveret.*

Fleck
Any feather or cape having specks or dotting that contrast with the hackle shade; probable origin of term may be Old Norse *flekkr* and others, meaning "flake" or "speck" (1750, *OED*).

Flue
The soft downlike fibers at the base of a feather; the down mass or feather itself; the soft, immature feather. The term comes from the Flemish *vluwe,* of the same meaning.

Fly board
Created by William Lunn, a fly board is a floating, wooden board that accumulates and protects insect eggs, thereby propagating such insects in rivers and streams. Various ephemerids oviposit on the underside of the tethered board, where the eggs later develop and hatch. "These are boards floating in the water, tethered to bridges or piles and posts, and the flies settle on the boards and go down to lay their eggs on the underside of

Section of fly board showing insect eggs and hatched nymphs

them, where caddis cannot get at them" (John Waller Hills, *River Keeper* [1934]). When covered with insect eggs (three deep according to Hills), the fly board may be transported to other reaches or other rivers that may require insect stocking.

Hills also described how Lunn made the fly board. Nail two rough deal boards together to prevent warping. Cut one end to a point and pass a wire through a hole in the point. Tether the board with a length of wire to a bridge or stake projecting from the bank. The point allows any weeds or debris to float by. Fly boards may have to be cleared occasionally of weeds, especially during a heavy weed cut. This unique method of insect propagation is still used on some English chalk streams.

Flymph

A fly-nymph pattern, an emerger; compare the soft-hackle fly and similar angling methods. Vernon S. Hidy coined the term *flymph* in 1963. Hidy, employing wet-fly concepts from James E. Leisenring, defined the term in "The Art of Fishing the Flymph," Part II of *The Art of Tying the Wet Fly & Fishing the Flymph* (1971): "Flymph—a wingless artificial fly with a soft, translucent body of fur or wool which blends with the undercolor of the tying silk when wet, utilizing soft hackle fibers easily activated by the currents to give the effect of an insect alive in the water, and strategically cast diagonally upstream or across for the trout to take just below or within a few inches of the surface film." Supposedly, flymphs suggest hatching insects, such as mayfly and caddis, as they struggle toward or drift just beneath the surface.

Forged bend

"A hammered or forged hook can be recognized by the flat sides of the bend" (Eric Taverner, *Fly-Tying for Salmon* [1942]). Mechanical forging was originally done by hammer blows. Forging hardens the metal and thickens the metal on the axis that will receive the most stress. Forging may increase the strength of a light-wire hook, such as a low-water salmon hook. Cold, flat forging may have limited value: The increased metal on one axis is at the expense of the metal on the other axis—metal that would have been bent anyway. What is gained on one axis is lost on the other. Forging may produce a more brittle bend without producing a significantly stronger bend. Forging may include part of the hook shank and spear as well as the bend. Modern forging is often mild and limited to the bend itself. See *Hook (nomenclature)*.

Foumart
See *Fitchew.*

Freestone river
A river, fed primarily by tributaries (from rain and snowmelt), that has a relatively steep gradient and that flows over loose, aggregate rocks or stones. Unlike a chalk-stream angler who "fishes the rise," a freestone angler usually "fishes the water." Because of the nature of the rapid, agitated water, a freestone fly pattern is usually visible (large or brightly colored), well hackled (buoyant), and, because the trout must quickly examine and select the pattern, suggestive rather than imitative. See *Chalk stream* for comparison.

Fur
Fur consists of several kinds of hairs. The *guard hairs* are straight and taper to a fine point. The *bristle* or *awn hairs* also taper to a fine point, but they are thinner than guard hairs and have a characteristic swelling just below the tip. Both the guard hairs and awn hairs are known as overhairs. The *underfur*—the down or wool hairs—are the thinnest of the hair types. The underfur has an even

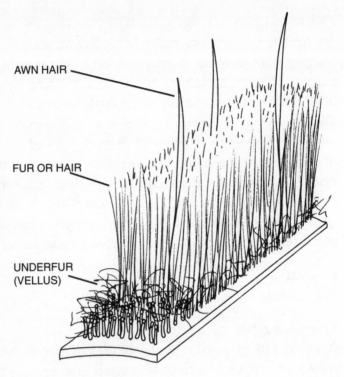

AWN HAIR

FUR OR HAIR

UNDERFUR
(VELLUS)

Fur patch

diameter throughout its length and is crimped or curvy.
The tightly crimped underfur acts as an insulator, and
the stiff overhairs create a protective shield to the soft
underfur.

Fur noodle

A dubbing technique and term popularized by Polly Rosborough in *Tying and Fishing the Fuzzy Nymph* (1969).
Create the noodle by "felting" chopped fur in warm,
soapy water. After rinsing and drying the fur mass, tease
out some, and roll it into a slender fur noodle, about 2½"
long and "the diameter of a wooden kitchen match." The
noodle is inserted in a dubbing loop, spun, and then
wrapped as fly body.

Furled

A leader or fly body twisted on its own axis. If one end of a cord or strand is spun and then folded so that both ends are together, it is apparent that the spin direction at each end coincides. With adequate spin, the cord will wrap or furl upon itself, producing a twisted cord that, when the ends are tied together, will not undo. This technique creates an extended fly body or a traditional tapered, furled leader.

Furnace hackle

A red or reddish-brown hackle with a black center or list. "Black centre and red edge is called Furnace" (G. E. M. Skues, *Silk, Fur and Feather* [1950]). Often confused with a coch-y-bondhu hackle, which has a black center and red barbs with *black tips*. A true furnace lacks the black-tipped barbs. Also a brown feather with a black center; a cape of furnace feathers.

Gallows

The gallows tool, also known as the Barlow gallows after the inventor, aids in tying the looped-stem parachute hackle. Bob Barlow, an English engineer working in Australia, created the gallows tool, which was later manufactured and marketed by John Veniard Limited of England. The concept is simple: A light spring tension holds the stripped and looped hackle stem, thus allowing the hackle to wrap around the looped stem to produce a knotted parachute hackle. After sufficient hackle turns, the hackle tip passes through the stem loop, and the gallows hook disengages. Both ends of the hackle stem are pulled taut to tie the parachute into a knot. Because the feather is self-knotted, the tying thread may be completely removed. The gallows tool, which also holds wing bundles or extended-body trusses, may be used for other tying methods. A gallows tool usually has (1) a vertical and horizontal adjustment to position the hanging hook or material clamp directly over the hook shank; (2) a soft

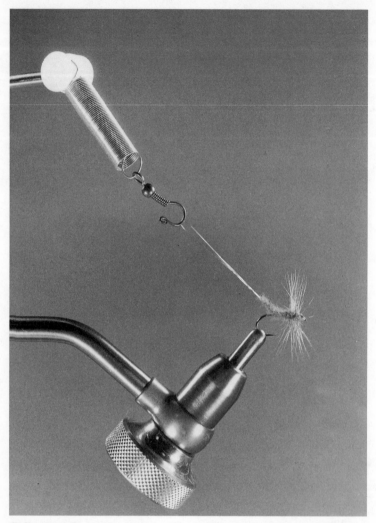

Gallows tool

spring that holds firmly, yet readily allows disengagement; (3) adequate free space around the vise head for hand and material movement; (4) a material clamp that adjusts for mounting extended-body patterns; and (5) a vise clamp that accepts standard vise-stem diameters and bends.

Gap

The distance across the hook bend between the hook point and the shank; also called gape (U.K.). See *Hook (nomenclature)*.

Gildard

The cast or tippet attached to the hook; variant of *gilder:* a snare, especially for small animals *(OED)*. "A 19th century *gildert,* for catching birds on snow, was a slip noose of horsehair tied to line" (Joseph T. Shipley, *Dictionary of Early English* [1968]). "The link of a line" (Thomas Best, *The Art of Angling* [1822]).

Gillaroo

An Irish brown trout with abundant red spots; literally, "the red fellow"; from the Irish *giolla ruadh* (*giolla,* lad, fellow and *ruadh,* red).

Gillie, ghillie

An angler's servant or boatman; Gaelic *gille,* lad, servant; Irish *giolla,* fellow; Gaelic *gille-casfliuch,* highland chief's follower; "specifically, the servant who carries the chief across streams" *(OED)*. See *Gillaroo*.

Gravid

Possessing fertile eggs; pregnant.

Greenwell

A ginger hackle with a black center; a ginger badger hackle. A Greenwell can have a pale red edge; however, if the edge is dark red, the hackle is often considered to be a furnace hackle, not a Greenwell hackle. The Greenwell was named after the hackle used in the Greenwell's Glory pattern first tied by the professional tyer James Wright of Sprouston in England and christened and popularized by Canon Greenwell of Durham, England. There is doubt as to the true originator. In *The Super Flies of*

Still Water (1977), John Goddard finds Mark Aitken's dressing earlier and similar to Greenwell's Glory. "A glorified Blue Dun" (Harold Smedley, *Fly Patterns and Their Origins* [1950]). An English term seldom encountered in American fly tying.

Grilse

A young Atlantic salmon that returns from the sea for the first time; a first-year, young salmon. Grilse generally weigh about 5 or 6 pounds, sometimes more. A grilse is called a salmon when it returns a second time to fresh water. When compared with a small salmon, "A grilse has smaller scales, which are very soft; also longer fins, and the tail more forked" (Richard Niven, *The British Angler's Lexicon* [1892]). G. W. Maunsell, in *The Fisherman's Vade Mecum* (1952), notes that "A grilse is more slender and graceful, has a smaller head, a more deeply forked tail; has thinner scales which come off more easily. A grilse after thirteen months in the sea will weigh 4 or 5 pounds, while after seventeen months it will weigh quite 10 pounds." According to the *OED,* the term is of unknown origin. Maunsell believes the term comes from the Swedish *gralax.* In Ireland, grilse is also known as *peal.*

Grizzly

The term *grizzly* comes from Middle English *grisel* and French *gris,* meaning gray; from the fourteenth to sixteenth centuries, a gray fur; the barred Plymouth Rock feather or cape; a bicolored feather with black or dark gray bars on a white, bluish-tinged field. According to the David Hawksworth's *British Poultry Standards* (1982), the points of excellence are straight bars, high contrast of bars, bar and ground color of equal widths, barring carried down into underfluff, and a black tip bar. The barred Plymouth Rock was first exhibited in 1869. The barred rock was developed, as an exhibition ideal, to secure the long, narrow, finely barred feather rather than body size or conformation. Note that the ground color is white, often with a bluish tinge, and the barring, which should be moderately narrow and straight, is a beetle-green black. Every feather should finish with a black tip. Also called *cuckoo,* a term derived from the breast markings of the European cuckoo. Frank Elder, in *The Book of the Hackle* (1979), maintains that the term *grizzly* should be used for the barred marking on the hackle rather than the hackle color—dun grizzly, ginger grizzly, or others. The Belgium campine has barred body feathers but not barred neck hackles. The dark cuckoo marans, from France, is black barred. The golden cuckoo marans has bluish gray hackles with gold and black bars. See *Cuckoo.*

Guard hairs

The long, stiff, and lustrous body hair of a fur bearer; the shield-shaped overhair of mammals. See *Fur.*

Gut

Gut or Paul Young's "cat gut" is a term derived from caterpillar gut, from the silk moth. According to John Waller Hills, "Silkworm gut is first mentioned by James Saunders in 1724 in the *Compleat Fisherman.*" Gut usually came in 12-inch to 15-inch lengths. Gut longer than 20 inches was rare. Gut lengths from 20 inches to 23 inches were in great demand to form the sections nearest the fly, hence the length of a traditional tippet. Gut formed not only the tippet lengths, but also the hook eye itself.

Modern tippet ratings (such as 3X, 4X) are based on drawn gut—gut drawn through a diamond hole. In the drawing process, one end of the gut was tapered with a revolving, abrasive wheel and then soaked in warm water. After the gut end entered the "funnel side" of the appropriate die opening, pliers then pulled the gut strand completely through the die hole. When the soaked gut was pulled through the hole, excess and irregularities were shaved off, and the strand came out roughly the same diameter from end to end. When considerable diameter reduction was required, several die sizes were used. There

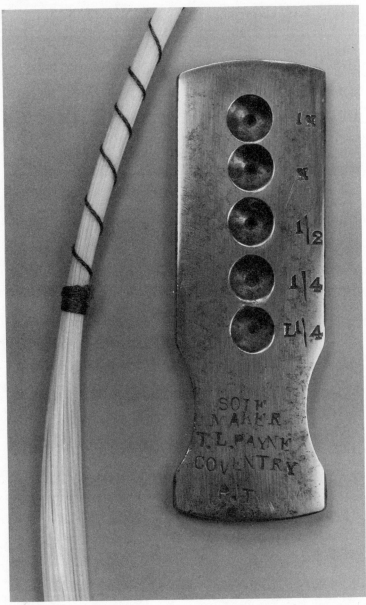

Gut and gut template

were usually five diamonds with different-sized holes mounted in a metal plate. The largest hole was approximately 0.0095 inch in diameter. Soft gut drawn through the largest hole was known as 1X gut. If a smaller size was wanted, it was drawn through the second diamond hole, shaving off more and making a smaller diameter—hence a 2X gut. This continued to the smallest 5X hole. The 6X diameter was available but not common. Notice that the larger the number, the smaller the diameter. Paul Young, in *Making and Using the Fly and Leader* (1935), lists the approximate inch diameter and the trade name of drawn gut. Note that the decimal number and the X number equals 10.

.005"—5X Drawn	.012"—Fina
.006"—4X Drawn	.013"—Regular
.007"—3X Drawn	.014"—Padron 2
.008"—2X Drawn	.016"—Padron 1
.009"—1X Drawn	.017"—Marana 2
.010"—Refinucia	.019"—Marana 1
.011"—Refina	.019"–20"—Imperial

Guttered

"A guttered hook is one that is cut with a file down each side of the barb, in order to remove any ragged edge left after the formation of the barb itself" (Eric Taverner, *Fly-Tying for Salmon* [1942]). Guttering creates a fine groove or "gutter" at the base of the barb, usually directed down in alignment with the rear edge of the barb.

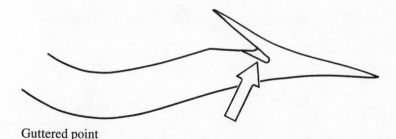

Guttered point

Hackle

The narrow, glossy feather on the dorsal cervical tract (back neck) of a bird; from Old English *hacele* or *haecile,* meaning "cloak" or "mantle"; a "hackle-fly," dated 1676 *(OED).* "An artificial fly, dressed with a hackle-feather, or something like this; a 'palmer.' Also hackle-fly. 1676" *(OED).* To dress a fly with a hackle feather, dated 1867 *(OED).* Other body feathers from a bird are the spey hackles (the long lateral sickle feathers at the tail base), the spade hackles (the wide shoulder hackles), and the saddle hackles (the dorsopelvic tract feathers), the long flank hackles between the spade hackles, and tail feathers. A feather mounted to imitate the wings or legs of insects.

Hackle gauge

In fly tying, a template or scale that measures the length of hackle barbs and indicates the proportionate hook size.

Hackle guard

In fly tying, a small cone-shaped disk that is placed over the eye of the hook to keep the hackle away from the whip-finishing process.

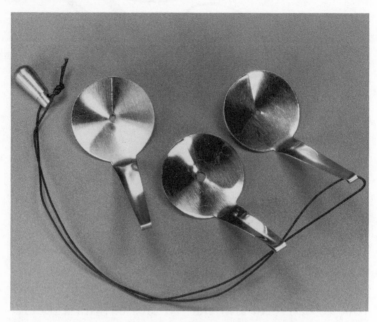

The slit in these cone hackle guards allows thread entry. A small weight (connected to a cord that passes through a hole in the vise stem) holds the guards in place. Once in place, the pattern may then be whip-finished without trapping any barbs.

Hackle pliers

In fly tying, a spring clip or clamp used to hold and ma-nipulate the hackle feather during mounting. Several shapes and sizes are available, many with a finger ring for ease of rotating the hackle around the hook shank. The traditional shape is that associated with Herb Howard pliers or Veniard's of England. Hackle pliers should hold firmly without cutting the hackle, be large

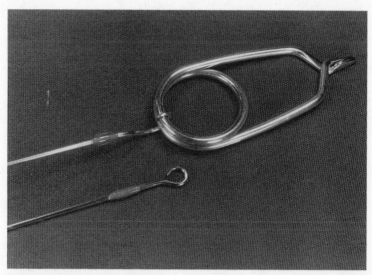

Standard English hackle pliers with removable spinning hook. A spinning hook swiftly spins the hackle pliers. Note also the tight hook-return on the standard thread spinner that spins a dubbing loop.

enough for handling, and have adequate weight "on the dangle." Hackle pliers may also be used to hold the tying thread during the tying process.

Most hackle pliers have the jaw axis at a right angle to the finger-hole axis; this encourages the hackle stem to twist during wrapping. Some modern hackle pliers have jaws that rotate independently, thereby decreasing hackle-stem twist. Such hackle pliers, however, lessen the tyer's total control over stem-twist. Hackle pliers should have (1) well-indexed jaws that hold securely without cutting; (2) adequate weight to maintain thread tension when on the dangle; (3) large and comfortable grip; (4) firm jaw tension with easy opening; and (5) size enough for comfort, yet compact enough for maneuvering.

Hair

Some hairs have specialized names such as fur (See *Fur*), fleece (the dense, soft hair of sheep), bristles (the short, stiff hairs of hogs), quills (the sharp, spiny hairs of porcupines and hedgehogs), and whiskers (the tactile hairs on various mammals). A flat hair shaft, which grows at an uneven rate, is curly; straight hair has a round shaft. Hair may be used in all parts of a fly pattern—tail fibers, dubbed body, wings, and legs or hackle.

Hair compactor

A cylindrical or disklike tying tool (with a slit or hole for the hook eye and shank) that compresses spun animal body hair radiating from the hook shank.

Hair compressor

A cylindrical tying tool for compressing bullet heads before wrapping the collar thread. See *Bullet head.*

A Delrin hair compactor

Hair Snare

A fly-tying tool that traps and positions various fibers for mounting on the hook.

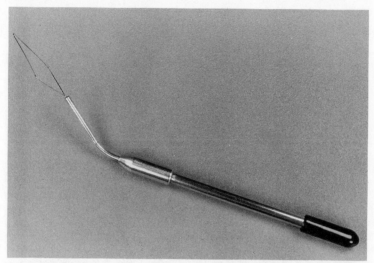

The original Hair Snare, made by Edgin Manufacturing, for capturing and holding various fibers during tying. By pulling the base cap, a wire loop closes and clenches any trapped fibers.

Hair stacker

A cylindrical tying tool that aligns the natural, tapered hair tips by gently tapping the tool on the table. There are two basic stacker designs: open and closed. A stacker has several features:

1. A small-bore chamber (0.250 inch to 0.437 inch) to bundle hairs. This is important when few hairs, such as those for tails, are stacked. A wide-bore stacker may allow the hairs to cross rather than to pile parallel. Large-bore stackers are useful when stacking crinkled or soft-tipped fibers. Crinkled or soft-tipped hairs, such as calf-tail hairs, are usually finger

stacked. Such fibers cling to each other, and their soft tips fold rather than align. A large-bore stacker, which *loosely* gathers the fibers, can align most of the fibers.

Matarelli hair stacker. Note the rubber base for cushioned tapping.

2. A positive grip and a wide, stable base cushioned for quiet tamping.
3. A smooth, nonstatic hair chamber.
4. A male lip of the hair chamber thick enough (0.060 inch or more) that the fibers are not disturbed when the female section withdraws.
5. A "free-bore" space between the bottom of the stacker and the male lip close enough (0.375 inch to 0.187 inch) to prevent the fibers from moving or falling during removal. In other words, the natural tips should be exposed enough for easy pickup, yet not so extended that they fall or touch the female wall during withdrawal from the base. After forceful stacking, several gentle 45-degree tapping strokes will channel the fibers together for pickup.

Half-hitch tool

A tapered tube that allows thread loops to slide off and form a locking head knot. If a series of single loops are used, usually head cement is added to make certain they will not unravel. A variation of the half hitch is a double or triple hitch. Instead of a single wrap around the half-hitch tube, two or three are made and passed over the fly head and tightened. This, in effect, produces a mini-whip that holds better than a single-loop hitch. See *Whip finisher.*

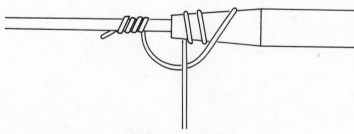

The three-wrap miniwhip with a half-hitch tool

Halford wings (basket wings)

In fly tying, an "Improved Method of Winging Upright Duns," advocated by Frederic M. Halford in *Floating Flies and How to Dress Them* (1886). This simple, practical method creates a compact wing base while avoiding wing-barb breaks.

1. First, create a thread base by overwrapping the forward third of the shank. Then select two matching wing panels. Cut them to width with stem sections attached. The attached stem sections lock the barbs together during mounting.

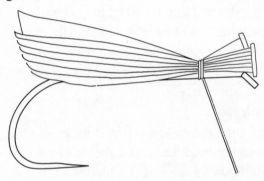

2. Mount the matched wings with the base pointing forward and front edge pointing up. Wing length should equal shank length. Pass two thread wraps over the wings to compress the barbs directly on top of the shank.

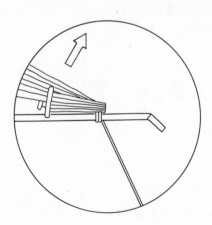

3. Then fold the winged stumps (the stemmed base) back on their respective sides and rotate the wing up.

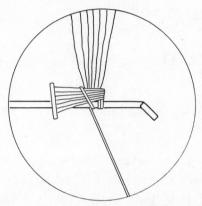

4. Wrap the thread directly behind the wings while erecting them. The wings are now caught in a "basket." The basket base should be kept as small as possible. Finally, for a smoothly tapered underbody, trim both wing stumps diagonally and overwrap with flat thread.

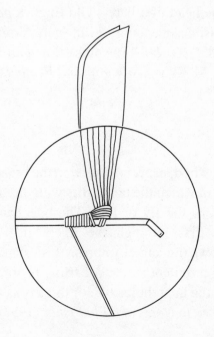

Halteres

Minute, knobbed appendages (halters) in place of the hind wings on Diptera; believed to be either vestigial wings or balancing knobs.

Hang a fish

"To hook a fish" (Thomas Best, *Art of Angling* [1822]).

Hare fleck

Dubbing from outside the shoulder of the hare.

Hare's flax

Dubbing from the leveret, a young, first-year hare. Hare's flax has reduced guard hairs, and is paler, shorter, and softer. G. P. R. Pulman, in *The Vade Mecum of Fly-Fishing for Trout* (1851), writes of "flax from the leveret's head and neck." Roger Woolley's Hare's Ear Dun, in *Modern Trout Fly Dressing* (1932), has "hare's flax tied in at the shoulder" for hackle. See *Flax.*

Hare's poll

Fur from the head of a hare. "Old English *poll* in place-names, possible meaning 'hill,' may originally have meant 'head' " *(OED).* "The pinky down fur between the ears" (G. E. M. Skues, *Silk, Fur and Feather* [1950]).

Harl

See *Herl.*

Harling

A trolling method, especially used in the broad Scandinavian rivers, in which the boat drifts with the current at the same speed as the fly or lure. The boatman guides the boat, stern first, through the likely fish zones. The method allows the angler to present flies and lures deep in heavy or turbulent water. A harling board, attached at the stern of the boat, holds two or three rods at the ready. W. S. Jackson, in *Notes of a Fly Fisher* (1933), rejects the

method as "giving you no opportunity for the employ-
ment of tactics" and, unlike trout fishing, being without
skill or knowledge. He describes harling as "sitting day
long facing the stern of a boat with two or three rods projecting behind, while two gillies slowly lower you down
the pools." The skill of the boatman, rather than the angler, is paramount. According to G. W. Maunsell, "You
must have a good boatman who knows the pools, banks,
channels, and the localities which fish frequent at the
various stages of the tide. Much depends on him" (*The
Fisherman's Vade Mecum* [1952]).

Harness, harnays
The harness. "The tackle, gear . . . , i.e. of a fishing-rod,
etc." *(OED)*. Equipment or accoutrements. "Ye shall vn-
derstand that the moost subtyll & hardyste crafte in
makynge of your harnays is for to make your hokis" (*The
Treatyse of Fysshynge wyth an Angle* [1496]).

Harry-long-legs
Commonly the cranefly (family Tipulidae) in older text,
not the Harvester (order Phalangida). Charles Cotton's
August Harry-long-legs had "the body made of Bear's
dun, and blue Wool mixt, and a brown Hackle-feather
over all." Charles Bowlker rejected the imitations, but
both George C. Bainbridge (*The Fly Fisher's Guide,* first
printed 1816) and Henry Wade ("Halcyon" [London,
1861]) list patterns.

Head hackle
Shoulder hackle.

Herl (herle, hurl, harl)
The long fuzzy barb of a peacock tail feather or ostrich
plume; a peacock tail feather strand. "A barb or fibre
of a feather, 1450" *(OED)*. "The herle of y pecok tayle"
(1496); a type of feather, such as peacock or ostrich herl,

with a specialized structure called a flue; from the Low German *harl,* meaning a filament or fiber of hemp or flax, hence "a herl of silk." "The body of copper-coloured peacock's harl" (Charles Bowlker, *The Art of Angling* [1839]). "The long plumelets or beards, called *herls,* of ostriches' and peacocks' feathers. . . ." (James Rennie, *Alphabet of Angling* [1849]).

Hipporus
See *Aelianus.*

Hog wool
"The soft down that is combed from the hog's bristles" (Izaak Walton, *The Complete Angler* [1766]). Pig's wool, "just the under hair of an ordinary pig" (George Leonard Herter, *Professional Fly Tying, Spinning and Tackle Making* [1971]). "Hogs Down. Be sure to procure from Butchers . . . Black, Red, Whitish and Sanded Hogs Down, such as is combed from the Roots of the Hair, or Bristles of Hogs of those Colours. . . ." (James Chetham, *The Angler's Vade Mecum* [1700]). "Of hair, there is none more useful than that called 'hog's down.' Naturally it is of various colours, and can be dyed of any hue advantageously. It resists water well, and when immersed in that element retains its vividness of colour, whatever that may be" ("Ephemera" [Edward Fitzgibbon], *A Handbook of Angling* [1848]).

James O'Gorman, in *The Practice of Angling* [1845]), emphasizes the need "to tease it out long and straggly." According to Richard Niven, "Hair adapted for fly dressing is principally got from the swine's belly, and is called pig's wool. It is a little coarse, and cannot well be used in the smaller or finer flies. It may be dyed any required colour. It stands the water remarkably well" (*The British Angler's Lexicon* [1892]). Seal hair, which was easier to dub, superseded hog's wool. According to

Resilient and lustrous hog wool dubbing

Fraser Sandeman, in *By Hook and By Crook* (1894), pig's wool was "far more brilliant in the water" than seal fur and "the fibres well assert themselves." The brittle fibers were usually broken to the required length and then applied to a well-waxed thread. Sandeman describes the preparation: "To prepare pig's wool, which can be purchased dyed in all shades, it is necessary to first clear it of the very coarse hairs and then break the remainder up in the fingers until the fragments are of required length, say in a medium size fly about ¼ of an inch, or longer for use towards the shoulder of the fly."

Hook bender
A small, nineteenth-century hand tool with template and pin that shaped the soft, pointed, and barbed hook wires into standard bends. Women and children, working at home, did piecework for such companies as Sealey, Allcock, and Partridge. The hook wire was trapped between the pin and template. The tool was rotated, which pressed the soft wire over the template and formed the bend. The

The handheld hook bender traps both barb and point so that the hook wire may be pulled or drawn into a prescribed shape.

shaped hook was then removed from the hook bender and returned to the company for forging, bowing (forming the eye), hardening, tempering, and bronzing. Hook bending "is quickly done by means of a small steel block around which the wire is bent, the shape of the block varying according to the particular bend required" (David Foster, *The Scientific Angler* [undated]). Foster regarded bending as a special operation that "decides the *shape,* and consequently, the particular species of hook to be produced."

Hook (nomenclature)
Usually a hook is selected by shank length (which matches the organism imitated) rather than gap size. In some patterns, however, gap size may be critical. Hooks numbered 2 through 28 grow smaller as the numbers increase; sizes 1 through 30/0 grow larger as the numbers increase. Only even-numbered hooks are commonly manufactured, although it may be possible to find elderly or modern odd-numbered hooks on occasion.

Basic Hook Terminology

1. *The shank:* That part of the hook from the rear of the eye to the beginning of the bend, usually a point directly above *the rear of the barb.* Rarely is the head space of the pattern (equal to the eye length of the particular hook) subtracted from the shank length. Although seldom adopted, the shank length may also be defined as the distance on the shank directly *above the hook point* to the rear of the hook eye (A. J. McClane (editor), *McClane's Standard Fishing Encyclopedia* [1965]).

2. *The bend:* The curved or bent section of the hook, which begins at the end of the shank and extends to the rear of the spear. See *Sproat, Limerick, Perfect bend, Sneck, Swan bend,* and *Flat bend.*

3. *The spear:* That portion of the hook from the bottom of the bend to the point tip.

4. *The throat:* The distance, parallel to the hook shank, from the front of the hook point to the farthest bend depth.

5. *The heel:* The lower half of the hook bend. That portion of the bend held by the fly vise.

6. *The point:* The front, tapered section of the spear.

7. *The barb:* The raised tine cut in the top of the spear, immediately behind the point. H. G. McClelland's *How to Tie Flies for Trout* (1939) discusses the Hardy "harpoon" hook, which had barbs cut into the near and far sides of the spear, and the Nicolay out-barb, with a barb cut into the underside of the spear.

Hook Variations

1. *Bends:* Perfect, Sproat, Limerick, and Sneck
2. *Shank length:* Regular, extra long, extra short
3. *Shank formation:* Straight, York, round, angled, "broken"
4. *Eye angles:* Up, down, ringed, blind

5. *Eye formations:* Looped ball, tapered, flat, vertical
6. *Wire diameters:* Regular, extra heavy, extra light
7. *Point formations:* Hollow, superior, cone, turned
8. *Offsets:* Kirbed, reversed
9. *Shank sections:* Regular, forged
10. *Shank tapers:* Regular, low-water
11. *Gap width*
12. *Spear length*
13. *Barbed* or *barbless*

When these hook variations are considered, it is no wonder that hooks appear in a thousand shapes and sizes. The following drawings illustrate various hook designs, traits, and terms.

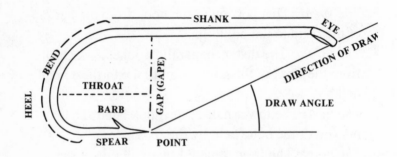

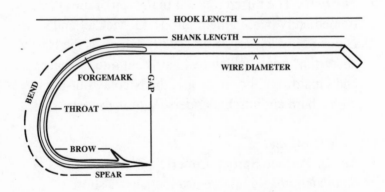

Hook nomenclature

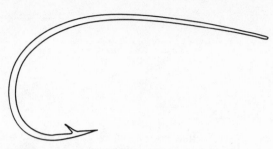

1662 hook from the frontispiece of *The Experienced Angler* by Robert Venables (1887).

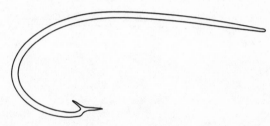

1789 hook used in fly tying by Thomas Cummess near Kilbreda (Kilbride) for Lough Mask (J. R. Harris, *An Angler's Entomology* [1939]).

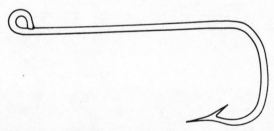

A vertical-eyed hook illustrated in J. March's *The Jolly Angler,* fourth edition, ca. 1842.

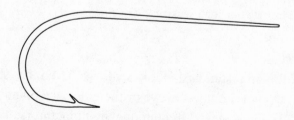

W. C. Stewart's loch and stream hook, ca. 1850s.

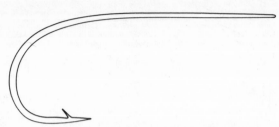

A graceful, tapered, blind hook from G. P. R. Pulman's *The Vade Mecum or Fly Fishing for Trout,* third edition, 1851.

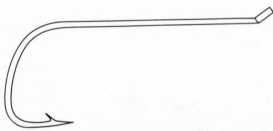

Dry-fly hook illustrated in Frederick M. Halford's *Floating Flies,* 1886.

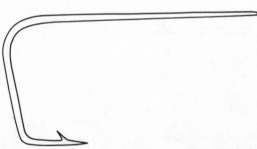

A North Country, blind and tapered, sneck-bend hook. John Bickerdyke's *The Book of the All-Round Angler,* ca. 1899. See also the pattern illustrated in John Jackson's *The Practical Fly-Fisher,* 1899.

Hook scale

The following standard hook scale is based on shank length. Do not include the eye or the gut space on antique hooks. Hook scales differ among manufacturers; there-

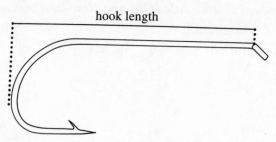

hook length

For hook length, omit the eye or the gut space on antique hooks.

fore, it is always more accurate to list the manufacturer as well as size and number, such as *Mustad 94840, size 14.* Many older hooks may be sized according to the "New Numbers" scale.

Standard Hook Scale (Old and New Designations)

Old Size Designation "Old Numbers"	Inches
8/0	2¾
7/0	2½
6/0	2¼
5/0	2
4/0	1⅞
3/0	1¾
2/0	1⅝
1/0	1½
1½	1⅜
1	1¼
2	1⅛
3	1
4	¹⁵⁄₁₆
5	¹⁴⁄₁₆
6	¹³⁄₁₆

Standard Hook Scale (Old and New Designations)

Old Size Designation "Old Numbers"	Inches	"New Numbers" (Trout Size)
7	¾	9
8	¹¹⁄₁₆	8
9	¹⁰⁄₁₆	7
10	⁹⁄₁₆	6
11	½	5
12	⁷⁄₁₆	4
13	¹²⁄₃₂	3
14	¹¹⁄₃₂	2
15	¹⁰⁄₃₂	1
16	⁹⁄₃₂	0
17	¼	00
18	⁷⁄₃₂	000

Horns

(1) The extended "ear flaps" at the base of a hackle cape, or (2) the matched barbs from the macaw's tail feather in a traditional salmon fly. See *Horns* under *Salmon fly (nomenclature)*.

Hyaline

A term used to describe the glassy, transparent wing of the mayfly spinner. From *hyal* or *hyalo*, "glass" from Greek *hyalos*.

Hypolimnion

See Epilimnion.

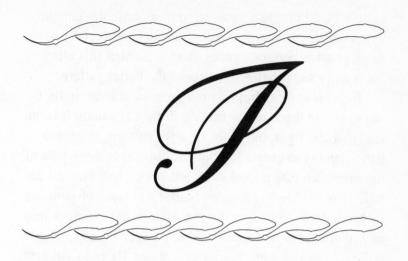

Imitation (the theory of fly-pattern imitation)

There are, of course, certain practical limitations imposed on the tyer, including the hook itself. Various factors, such as skill, materials, and methods, govern a tyer's approach to the craft. The possible variations in fly tying, as in other arts, create various "schools," ranging from the purely nonfunctional deconstructions to the superrealistic patterns. These extremes usually create patterns for art rather than for fish.

An insect may be imitated or represented in various ways. To give some insight into what is meant by imitation, fly patterns may be classified according to the following categories: impressionism, fancy, realism, deconstruction, and caricature. Traditionalism, which imitates an historic ideal rather than an insect, should also be included. These terms, like all abstract terms, are prone to vagueness and misuse. Nevertheless, the categories are serviceable with respect to the intentions and specific aesthetic aims of the tyer. Seldom, if ever, will a particular pattern be a complete expression of a particular category. Tyers may even scramble categories in a particular pattern to emphasize certain aspects. And it is often this alloy of ideas and exaggeration that proves the better pattern.

Impressionism: Impressionism is an attempt in fly tying to create the visual sensation of the organism: It is the study of the light and color of a fly pattern. Impressionism attempts to create the optical illusion or sensation of the organism rather than strict adherence to form and detail. This is akin to Georges Seurat's system of painting in small dots—dots that the eye blends and arranges into new colors and new forms. When a tyer blends various colors to create new colors or creates flash to suggest life, he creates the seductive sensation of the organism. It is argued that multicolored hackles, such as cree, may produce the "blurred sensation" of wing movement. For the impressionist, insect detail and texture need not be imitated.

Although Frederic M. Halford belonged to the "exact imitation" school, his emphasis on color over size and shape places him closer to the impressionists than the realists. The *raison d'être* of *Modern Development of the Dry Fly* (1923) was "an attempt to reproduce in the artificial flies the exact shades and tones of colour of the natural insects they are intended to counterfeit." His influence came from his friend and colleague, Edgar Williamson. Williamson "had for many years been a firm believer in the paramount importance of reproducing in each part of the artificial fly the precise shade of colour of the same part of the natural insect, and at the same time dressing a fly as nearly as possible of the exact size and shape of the living subimago and imago." To Halford, if an insect's body and thorax were different colors or shades, then "their relative proportions can be noted and reproduced." Even the turbinate eyes of the male spinner, often a bright yellow, orange, or red, can be imitated by two or three turns of dyed horsehair.

Impressionism is expressed in tying more through trout eyes than through man's. Since chapter 1 of Alfred Ronalds's *The Fly-Fisher's Entomology* (1844), trout perception has guided the tyer. A pattern should produce the same sensation that the natural insect produces. Early angling writing was merely an expression of the contemporary scientific discussions of light and optics. It was Vincent Marinaro's *In the Ring of the Rise* (1976) that drew the American angler's attention to the refraction theory. Marinaro's peek through the trout's window became the basis for two tying codes: "the artificial dun pattern must be kept above the surface film" and "anything that breaks through the surface film is no longer obscured by the oblique rays or the diffusion above the film." A pattern should not receive undue scrutiny by selective trout.

Brian Clarke and John Goddard, in *The Trout and the Fly* (1980), modernized our knowledge of trout perception and, like Marinaro, created patterns based on the trout's impression of the natural. For example, the authors emphasized two sensations produced by the dun that they believed were "key triggers" to the rise: "the star-burst of dimples created by the feet of the naturals" and the wings' penetration into the trout's ring of vision. In the case of the spinner, the authors advocated pockmarked polyethylene wings that "come close to transmitting the correct light pattern below the surface."

The Shadow Mayfly, a Peter Deane pattern based on a dressing from J. Arthur Palethorpe of Berkshire, has no body, only a grizzly palmer and brown hackle wing stubs. This impressionistic pattern, first fished on the Kennet, consistently seduces selective trout on England's chalk streams. Gary LaFontaine's Emergent Caddis incorpo-

Impressionism: the Sparkle Pupa tied by Gary LaFontaine

rates an impressionistic blend of fur and sparkle for a variegated vibrancy of life. LaFontaine, an avowed impressionist, imitates the bright bubble sheath of the ovipositing female caddis with bright, reflective Antron yarn.

Fancy: In fly tying, a fancy pattern is the vague notion that a fly pattern is basically a tyer's idea of what is imitated. Materials, usually arranged in a decorative manner, capture a concept rather than the creature. Fancy patterns appear neither in nature nor in the impressions of nature. They are, instead, products of the imagination or fancy. Such patterns are often original and extravagant blends of methods and materials. Some of the exotic salmon patterns and whimsical "attractors" may be stuck in the fancy wallet. They are more the result of imagination and the subjective response than imitation. If this is the application of "the fallacy of misplaced reality," then tying is only the richer for it.

Although remnants of "attraction" and "impressionism" appear, James Rennie's *Alphabet of Angling* (1849) illustrates a "fanciful" salmon fly imitation of an adult dragonfly. For Rennie, fish may be so capricious that they prefer a fancy fly instead of a natural or realistic imitation. He notes that "The aim of the angler accordingly ought to be to have his artificial fly calculated, by its form and colours, to attract the notice of the fish, in which case he has a much greater chance of success than by making the greater efforts to imitate any particular species of fly." Fish may be more deceived by the "appearance" of life and motion than by the specific resemblance to any natural creature. Rennie concludes that the artificial fly ought to attract by "form and color."

Rennie's Imitative Dragonfly

The detailed, ultrarealism of Bill Logan's stonefly nymph. The edge of the hook eye becomes the labrum.

Realism: In fly tying, a realistic pattern imitates, usually with some detail, the actual insect or trout food. Most "representational" patterns force the eye to complete what the pattern implies: Tying halts short of the natural, short of microscopic reality. Realistic tying usually involves a closer examination of the natural, more detail, and more parts. Few tyers would maintain that a fly should be an exact copy of nature—a nature that is remarkably subtle and cryptic in the insect world. And few tyers, perhaps only the extreme expressionists, would claim that a pattern should have no relationship with nature. But realism too has dimensions.

Ultrarealistic or "supernatural" tying may be akin to model building. Indeed, such patterns are often tied for the wall, not the water. So much care may be devoted to each tying step that the procedure itself may engross the tyer. All tying is not utilitarian.

Traditionalism: The traditional tyer, using the original materials (when available) and methods, accurately

Nadica and Igor Stančev of Skopia, FYR Macedonia, are competitive fly-tyers. European fly-tying competitions have produced remarkable tying realism. Nadica and Igor are among the finest tyers in Europe. The Danica Dun depicted above was tied by Nadica Stančev.

"copies" a traditional pattern, the authoritative source. Color, proportion, and symmetry are to an historic ideal rather than to an insect or a private theory. As C. F. Walker noted in *Fly-Tying as an Art* (1957), the traditionalists "are, as a rule, merely copying copies, rather than imitating flies." Tying such patterns, which are prescriptive and formal, does give the tyer a sense of ritual and historic continuity. This is not necessarily thoughtless prescriptive tying; the past is rich in patterns that can challenge the devoted and diligent tyer. Just collecting rare and unusual materials can be an adventure. There is also the problem of the text reliability and text interpretation. Fernando Basurto, in *Dialogue* (1539), tells the reader to "turn the feathers back towards the hook in such a way that they hide it all the way to the end of the point." Is this merely hook-length reversed wings or wings draped beneath the shank that cover the hook point? What does *it* refer to? Even literal readings may be ambiguous. In the *Treatyse* (1496), are the partridge feathers on the Dun Fly and Ruddy Fly *hackles* (John Waller Hills) or merely *clump wings* (John McDonald)?

Deconstruction: Steve Fernandez of California defines his approach as modern "deconstruction." Some patterns are more experiments in aesthetics than in fishing tackle. His tying, however, suggests a possible modern tangent of tying. His *Untitled, 1983* is a "deconstruction" of an Atlantic salmon pattern tied on a *straightened* hook. The result is a unique *unfly*. "This work is reminiscent of the work of Dada artists. The idea is to break from tradition and throw out all conventions in order to create something completely new. Since traditional featherwing flies are now considered art—I created art. Absolutely not fishable; the hook is straightened out. The traditional materials are placed on the hook at quite atypical positions."

Fernandez's *Pompadour 1987* is a more conservative blend of popular art, tarnished materials, and hairstyle combined with traditional Dee Atlantic salmon tying. Furthering the concept of the *Pompadour 1987* is the "radical deconstruction" work *Untitled* (ca. 1991). Fernandez describes this approach and pattern: "A feather represents the 'hook.' The topping is tied on under the hook and behind the wing, echoing its form and extending in front of the hook. The sides (a rarely used portion of the jungle cock feather) become, by manipulation, sides and throat. All materials are then tied onto the pointed stainless steel wire at different and 'out of sequence' locations."

Caricature: The caricaturist exaggerates some feature (a feature considered essential) at the cost of other

Pompadour 1987

features. Baigent's Variant, for example, has an extended, exaggerated hackle that was believed to mimic the optical effects of a floating insect.

Impressionism
See *Imitation*.

Incomplete metamorphosis
The physical changes in the development of an insect that include ovum, nymph, and adult.

Indian grass, weed
A plant material used for hook strands or lines. Sir Izaak Walton writes: "Indian, or Sea-grass makes excellent Hook links; and though some object to it, as being apt to grow brittle, and to kink in using, with proper management it is the best material for the purpose yet known. . . ." Walton endorses Indian grass, concluding that "If your grass is coarse, it will fall heavily in the water, and scare away the fish; on which account gut has the advantage. But, after all, if your grass be fine and round, it is the best thing you can

use" (Walton, *The Complete Angler* [1766]). Walton recommends preparing the grass by laying it in scummed fat for 3 or 4 hours, stripping off the excess fat and then storing the grass in a well-oiled bladder. Before use it should be soaked in water for a half-hour, or, during the walk to the riverside, moistened in the mouth. In James Chetham's *The Angler's Vade Mecum* (1700), an advertisement claims that "East India Weed" proves "so strong and fine, of a water colour, that it deceives the Fish much more than Hair or Silk." According to John Waller Hills in *A History of Fly Fishing for Trout* (1971), this is the first mention of Indian grass. Although this "Oriental" plant appeared throughout the eighteenth century, it has yet to be identified.

Insect (nomenclature)

The following insect nomenclature is commonly used in taxonomy and, to a lesser extent, in fly tying.

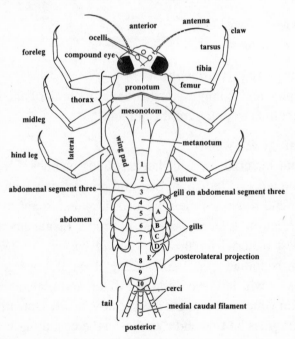

Basic insect nomenclature (mayfly nymph)

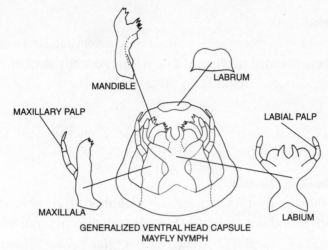

Generalized ventral head capsule (mayfly nymph)

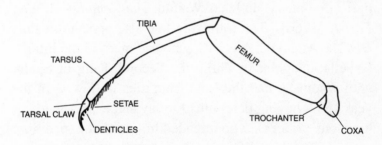

Insect leg nomenclature

Instar
The immature insect during a stadia (see *Stadia*) between molts; such nymphs are further classified as junior (immature) or senior (mature) instars; a term for the period between molts.

Integument
The skin of an insect. See *Exuvia*.

Intercalary
See *Marginal intercalary veins*.

Interstitial

Occurring in interstices, a small or narrow space between objects; located in a crevice or fissure; usually said of insect habits and insect body parts.

Irons

Early Scottish term for salmon hooks. Sometimes used as a general term for any large fish hook.

Isabella (colored)

A color of fly-tying material. "Dubbing of an absolute Black mix'd with 8 or 10 Hairs of Isabella coloured Mohair . . . " James Chetham, *The Angler's Vade Mecum* [1700]). "A kind of whitish yellow, or, as some say, buff colour a little soiled" (Charles Cotton, quoting from "Altieri's dictionary" in Izaak Walton, *The Complete Angler, Part II* [1766]). The following tale also appears in *Part II:* "The Archduke Albertus, who had married the Infanta Isabella, daughter of Philip the Second, King of Spain, with whom he had the Low Countries in dowry, in the year 1602, having determined to lay siege to Ostend . . . his pious princess, who attended him in that expedition, made a vow, that till it was taken she would never change her cloaths *[sic]*. Contrary to expectation, as the story says, it was three years before the place was reduced, in which time her Highness's linen had acquired the above mentioned hue" (Izaak Walton, *The Complete Angler* [1766]).

Jack

"Name of animals (sometimes signifying *male*, sometimes *small, half-sized*)" *(OED)*. The male mayfly *(Ephemera danica)*. "The one [mayfly] represented is the female; the male, or Jack, as he is called, being much smaller, his wings shorter than his body, and his colour much darker" (John Jackson, *The Practical Fly Fisher* (1899). In *Part II* of *The Complete Angler* (1766), Charles Cotton calls the emergent adult stonefly a *Jack:* "But so soon as ever they begin to put out, that he feels himself strong, at which time we call him a Jack, squeezes himself out of prison, and crawls to the top of some stone." "A young or small pike (1587)" *(OED)*. "With regards to taking Jacks with a fly, I am not able to say anything from my own experience; but I see no reason why they should not rise to one of a very large size, made of gaudy materials, so as to entice" (Captain T. Williamson, The *Complete Angler's Vade Mecum* [1808]).

Jam knot

A simple knot for attaching gut to an eyed hook. "There is a jam knot attaching eyed hooks to the casting line. Push one end of gut through the eye towards the bend of the hook; bring it back and make with it a slip knot round the line; don't draw this slip knot tight, leave it so open that it will pass over the eye of the hook, which is done by pulling on the main line; it then tightens and the knot is complete" (Richard Niven, *The British Angler's Lexicon* [1892]).

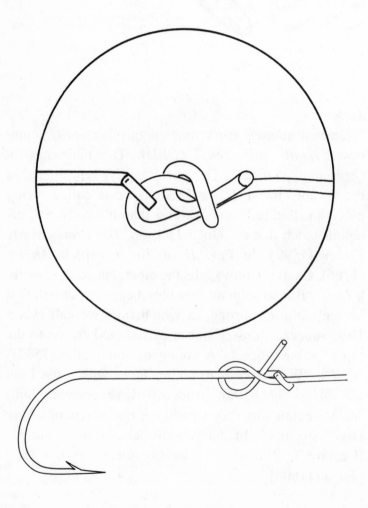

Keel hook

A hook bend, popularized by Dick Probst, characterized by an offset shank designed to produce a "weedless" hook. The dressed keel hook floats with the hook point up, opposite to the traditional float attitude.

Kelly kettle

The ingenious Kelly kettle, which boils water within minutes, allowed the Irish angler to have his tea even in wind and rain. Based on an original turn-of-the-previous-century design, the Kelly kettle was first made by a Tipperary tinker and angler named Kelly, given name unknown. Much later, in the early 1980s, another Kelly—a certain Padraic Kelly—traveled Ireland to study the various Kelly designs; he now holds the patent for the modern Kelly kettle. Looking much like a small volcano, the Kelly is light, compact, and remarkably efficient. The bottom inverts, creating a ventilated firebox. The tapered water chamber wraps water around the fire for rapid heating. The inner fire chamber is charged with twigs, dry grass, twisted newspaper logs, or kindling. Once ignited, the flame generates a rolling boil in about 3 minutes. For increased draught and a roaring fire, the base vent can be faced into the wind. For travel, the kindling and paper may be stored inside the kettle. The fire is completely contained during heating, and a handle and

Modern Kelly kettle with base inverted, creating the firebox.

chain provide easy pouring. Any excess water douses the fire when done.

Kick

"Kick in a fly is usually made by turns of silk behind the hackle to make each fibre stand out" (G. W. Maunsell, *The Fisherman's Vade Mecum* [1952]). Skues advocated kick in hackled wet flies. Without kick, the fly is dead: "With it, it is alive and struggling; and the fly which is alive and struggling has a fascination for the trout which no dead thing has." Skues created kick by whip-finishing behind the hackle and then varnishing the whip. The hackle barbs stood out from the pattern and moved in the current.

Kirby

A hook bend characterized by a semiangular shape and an offset where the point is turned away from the bend plane. The Kirby offset points to the left when the bend is up and the point faces you. The opposite bend, where the offset points to the right, is a reversed bend. Although the Kirby hooks, originated by Charles Kirby of London, are not common, they are excellent for small wet patterns. See *Sneck*.

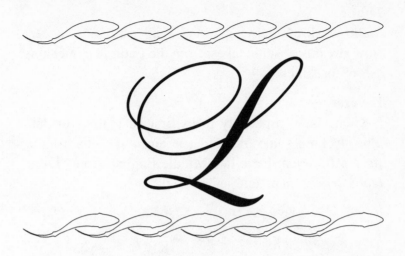

Labrum
The upper or front lip of an insect.

Larva
The immature, developmental stage, between the egg and the pupa, of an insect that undergoes a complete metamorphosis; the larval stage with several or numerous instars precedes the pupal, adult, or subimaginal stage, depending on the insect; plural, larvae. See *Instar.*

Leash of fish
Three fish (Thomas Best, *The Art of Angling* [1822]).

Legginess
Ultrasoft, high-tack dubbing waxes may "lick" or "string," i.e., stretch like taffy, when applied along a thread. A modicum of "legginess," so known in the adhesive trade, permits easy application of the dubbing wax to the thread. Merely stroke the thread smooth if excessive legginess appears on the tying thread.

Lentic

Static or slowly moving water; said in relation to very slow streams or static lakes; from the Latin *lent,* meaning "slow" or "thick."

Leveret

A young hare, especially in its first year; the soft dubbing, lacking some of the dense and thick guard hairs, from a first-year hare; late Middle English from "Latin, *lepus, lepor-* 'hare' and -et" *(OED).*

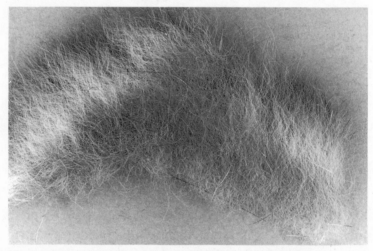

Fine, soft leveret fur ranging from dark gray to pale cream.

Limerick

A hook characterized by an acutely angled bend where the sharpest curve is at the rear of the spear. The bend merges imperceptibly with the shank. Because of the mechanically weak acute bend and streamer use, the hook is usually made from heavy wire. The Limerick salmon hook is often bronzed rather than japanned. The advantages include attractive "rakish" lines, a hook that "trails" well in heavy water, and a setback point that produces a

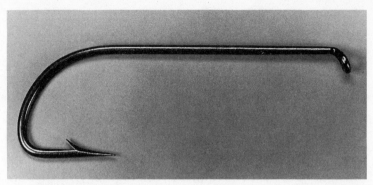

Limerick hook bend

superior penetration angle. The disadvantages include a sharp bottom bend that is considered by some to be less strong than bends with a rounded heel. The abruptness of the bottom bend varies among manufacturers. Although the angular bend may gather more mechanical stress, the heavier wire of salmon and streamer hooks produces a strong bend. Another disadvantage is the significant extension of steel beyond the body of the fly, which may be a factor in rejection. However, the trailing feathers and fibers of some wets and streamers may conceal the bend and point. The term *Limerick* is often attributed to the town in Ireland.

Listing
The term is correctly applied to the center or lateral strips running on each side of the feather stem that are darker than the rest of the feather; also used for any feather or hackle, regardless of color, that has a black edge or list without a black center. List is sometimes used only for the black edge of the barbs; a furnace has a black list with red margins, and a badger has a black list with silver or white margins. The demarcation of color is the margin between the barbs and the barbules

of the feather. Term origin is from Old English, *liste,* meaning border, edging, or strip. The general meaning was established by 1696. As it has come to mean both a band as well as an edge, the term has appeared in angling history as a feather with either a dark center strip or a dark edge strip. Eric Partridge's *Origins* (1983) defines list as "an edge or border," which derives from Old High German *lista,* meaning a strip or border. Walshe's *A Concise German Etymological Dictionary* (1956) suggests the origin in the Latin *litus,* seashore or border of the ocean. "*Lyste,* a stripe" (Thomas Satchell, *Glossary* to *Treatyse of Fysshynge Wyth an Angle* [1883]).

Loop-rod

Term popularized by David Webster's *The Angler and the Loop-Rod* (1885). ". . . A two-handed spliced rod, measuring from 13 feet 6 inches to 13 feet 8 inches. It consists of three pieces. The butt is made of ash, the middle piece of hickory, and the top of lancewood. When greater lightness is desired, lime tree may be used for the butt: what the rod gains in this respect, however, is lost in durability. Attached to the extremity of the top piece is a strong loop of twisted horse-hair, through which is passed the loop of the hair-line used in casting." The loop-rod, sans reel, was thus characterized by the horsehair loop at the tip. The horsehair casting line was about 18 to 20 feet long, tapering from thirty-six to forty-five hairs at the butt to five or six hairs at the gut. The gut line extended 16 to 17 feet, thus creating a total line length (from line loop to tail fly) of 34 to 37 feet. Nine flies, on 2-inch looped droppers, were attached to the gut line.

Lotic

Moving, as in lotic water, such as a stream or river.

Portrait of David Webster with loop-rod (*The Angler and the Loop-Rod* [1885])

Low-water fly

A lightly dressed salmon fly with wing tips well forward of the hook bend. Low-water patterns, for summer or low-water conditions, are usually fished with the greased-line method. Traditionally, the fly line and leader, within about 18 inches of the fly, were dressed to float while drifting the fly within a few inches beneath the surface. Today standard dry-fly lines are normally used. See *Salmon fly (types)*.

Lug

The ear (chiefly Scottish and Northern dialect); as in the pattern Hare Lug for Hare's Ear. Hare lug, "Down from the outside of the hare's ear" (W. H. Lawrie, *Scottish Trout Flies* [1966]). "A good hare-lug will provide body-material for several dozen flies, and that of various shades and complexions, from a swarthy black on to a dingy white. The back or furry part of the ear, however, is that which, in point of colour, is most acceptable to the fly-dresser" (Thomas Tod Stoddart, *The Angler's Companion* [1853]).

Magazine

A bag, satchel, or pouch for storing fly-dressing materials. "A pouch, bag, wallet, usually of leather, 1432" *(OED).* "A portable receptacle for articles of value, now rare, 1768" *(OED).* "The Angler must always have in readiness

Copperplate engraving of *Piscator* tying a fly. Note the magazine held by the youth and the light entering through the open window for tying. Early prints of this copperplate may constitute the first depiction of fly tying (Izaak Walton, *The Complete Angler* [1766]).

a large Magazine Bag, or Budget plentifully furnished"
(James Chetham, *The Angler's Vade Mecum* [1700]).

Magazine pliers

An ordinary hackle pliers with a small metal spool
clipped within the frame. The spool holds tinsel, silk, or
tying thread that may be gripped by the jaws at any time.
Especially useful for silks and metal tinsels that soil or
tarnish readily. T. R. Henn, in *Practical Fly-Tying*
(1950), refers to magazine pliers.

Mandibles

The outer or paired jaws of an insect. See *Insect (nomenclature)*.

Marabou

The fluffy, immature turkey feather. The "blood feather"
is the long, underdeveloped feather with barbs parallel to
the feather stem. Such feathers are often 3 or 4 inches
long. The term comes from the similar long fluffy feather
from the marabou stork.

Marginal intercalary veins

The unconnected veins, single or double, at the outer
margins (the trailing edge) of an insect's forewing.

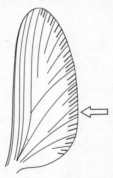

Marginal intercalary veins on the trailing edge of a mayfly wing.
The family Baetidae has short, single or double intercalary veins.
The genus *Baetis* has double intercalary veins. Genus *Centroptilum*
and genus *Cloeon* have single intercalary veins. The family
Leptophlebiidae has connected (attached) intercalary veins.

Marrying

The joining of different wing sections by engaging the hook projections. Barb panels from different feathers are joined together to form a new and complete wing section. The married panels are used primarily for mixed and built-wing salmon flies. See *Feather (nomenclature)*.

Mayfly

The aquatic insect classified as the order Ephemeroptera, meaning "short-lived winged" insect (*ephemero*, "for a day," "short-lived;" and *ptera*, "winged"), hence "lasting but a day," also called "dayfly." The English term *mayfly* was so given because of the major appearance of particular insects during the month of May; also called drake (see *Drake*). The mayfly develops from ova to nymph to dun (subimago) to spinner (imago), and finally to spent spinner. The mayfly is the only insect to "hatch" or molt again (from dun to spinner) after emergence. This final molt is sometimes known as the "bush hatch." Mayfly nymphs are often classified by the angler according to habitat adaptations as swimmers, burrowers, clingers, crawlers, and sprawlers.

Mayfly Nymph Characteristics (junior and senior instars)
1. Three distinct body parts: head, thorax, and abdomen
2. Three tails, except for one genus *(Epeorus)* and one species *(Baetis bicaudatus, bi* = two, *cauda* = tail)
3. Two short antennae
4. One pair of wing pads
5. Platelike or leaflike gills on the top or sides of abdomen
6. Ten abdominal segments
7. Six legs, each with a single claw
8. Significant variety in size and shape

Dun Characteristics (the subimago)
1. Gray or gray-brown wings with or without markings
2. Lack of mature coloration of body and wings
3. Two or three threadlike tails
4. Large front wings, held erect or saillike, and smaller or absent hind wings
5. Small, bristlelike antennae

Spinner Characteristics (the imago)
1. The sexually mature adult
2. Often has elongated front wings
3. Glassy, hyaline (transparent) wings that may or may not have contrasting marks
4. Terminal claspers for mating (males)
5. Tails may equal their dun length (males)
6. Development of complete coloration after 6 to 8 hours

In fly tying, the imitative elements of the mayfly include wing and body shape, size, and color. More realistic patterns may also imitate tail color and approximate length. Traditionally, the hackle imitates either wing or leg color of the insect.

Mayfly nymph

Adult mayfly

Mayle

The mayle feather; the barred or finely etched breast feathers, suggesting chain-mail armor: "The breast-feathers of a hawk when the feathers are full grown. Occasionally applied to the plumage of other birds" 1486 *(OED)*. "Having breast-feathers (of a specific colour)" 1575 *(OED)*. "The whitest mayle [feather] of the wylde drake" (*The Treatyse of Fysshynge Wyth an Angle* [1496]). "Speckled feathers; the Latin *macula* became *maille* in Old French" (Thomas Satchell's glossary in *An Older Form of The Treatyse of Fysshynge Wyth an Angle* [1883]).

Microbiota

Microscopic organisms not visible to the unaided eye.

Microcaddis (order Trichoptera)

The term *microcaddis* may refer to any small caddisfly, especially those ranging from 2 to 6 millimeters. However, the term should apply only to the true microcaddis, the Hydroptilidae. There are fourteen genera in North America. The most important are *Hydroptila,*

Leucotrichia, Oxyethira, and *Ochrotrichia.* The genus *Hydroptila* is common in most trout waters.

Microcaddis Larva Characteristics
1. Size: 2–5 millimeters
2. Body color: yellow, brown, or olive

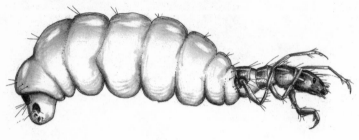

Microcaddis larva *(Hydroptila)*

3. Larvae are free living. They build no case until the fifth or final instar. Then they build a slipper- or bottle-shaped case (*Hydroptila* and *Ochrotrichia*) made from fine sand or parchmentlike silt *(Leucotrichia).*

Adult Microcaddis Characteristics
1. Size: 2–5 millimeters
2. Body color ranges from yellow to brown to green with tan or black mottled wings
3. Antennae relatively short, about half of body length

Adult microcaddis *(Hydroptila)*

4. Hind wing narrow and pointed with posterior fringe of long, fine hairs

In fly tying, the adult imitative elements include size, color, and down wings. Wings are often flat rather than the typical tent shape. Many adult microcaddis have a hairy or fuzzy appearance.

Midge

A generic term used to describe any minute insect; the term is related to the Latin *musca,* meaning "fly": The term usually and more correctly refers to the Chironomid. The larger Chironomids are often called "buzzers"—the English term—or gnats. Some English anglers reserve the term *midge* just for the terrestrial diptera, *Biblio johannis.* However, in general angling usage, the midge has come to mean any of a variety of minute insects including Chironomids, reed smuts, black gnats, buffalo gnats, black flies, and dixa midges, as well as microcaddis and other microinvertebrates, including tiny terrestrials. Ed Koch, in *Fishing the Midge* (1972), defines *midge* as "an artificial imitation of any small aquatic or terrestrial insect that a trout would find acceptable as food." See *Chironomid.*

Miller's Thumb

The Bullhead, muddler, or sculpin; a small, freshwater fish of the genus *Cottus;* an important trout food. "The head of the fish has some resemblance to a thumb" 1440 *(OED).* In the Middle Ages, millers were notorious for their "thick thumbs" that pressed on the grain scales to cheat their customers. This is why Geoffrey Chaucer's miller, in the *Prologue* to *The Canterbury Tales,* "hadde a thombe of golde." "The Miller's Thumb or Bull-head, is a fish of no pleasing shape. He is by *Gesner* compared to the Sea-toad-fish, for his similitude and shape. It has a

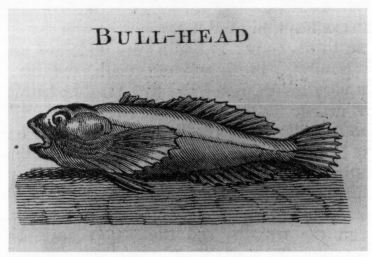

Illustration of the Bullhead or Miller's Thumb in the Hawkins edition of *The Complete Angler* (1766)

head, big and flat, much greater than suitable for his body; a mouth wide and usually gaping" (Izaak Walton, *The Complete Angler* [1766]).

Mirror
See *Window.*

Mixed wing
A salmon fly wing that is formed from different feather panels married to form a single, complete wing. See *Salmon fly (types).*

Moccoda, mockado
From the Italian *mocaiardo mohair (OED).* "A kind of cloth much used for clothing in the 16th and 17th century" *(OED)*; appears in fly tying about 1543 *(OED)*; fustian, type of inferior material *(OED)*. "Then I take a worsted thread, or moccoda end" (Robert Venables, *The Experienced Angler* [1827]). Geoffrey Chaucer's knight in the *Prologue* to *The Canterbury Tales* wears a jerkin

of "fustian cloth," occasionally defined as a cheap, rough cotton.

Moon

The Mee Moon—created by Mike Mee of Yorkshire, England—is an adjustable disk or shield that is placed behind the fly for contrast, making the viewing and tying easier. The moon is especially effective for tying small patterns. Some moons offer interchangeable neutral gray or green and cream disks—a different color on each side—for contrast. The adjustable moon prevents glare while allowing a clear, contrasting view of fine barbs and thread work. Some moons connect to the vise stem with an angled arm and slip-clamp and have complete articulation of the arm for positioning. Like a real moon, the disk "orbits" the vise shaft to offer an adjustable background for tying.

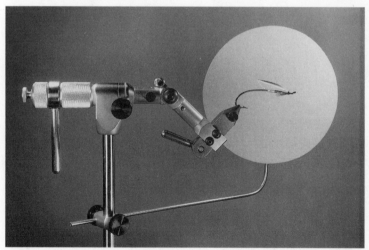

An adjustable moon attached to a vise stem. Notice the contrast between the fly pattern and the moon disk.

Naiad

Any aquatic nymph; also *naid,* from the Greek mythological river spirits. Compare Old French *noiant,* from Latin, *nare,* "to swim."

Natant

The floating or swimming insect stage, especially floating on the surface of the water; the emergent nymphal stage. The term is related to the Latin *nare*, meaning "to swim." See *Naiad.*

Notum

The dorsal plates of a thorax, said of insects.

Nymph

The immature stage of an insect having an incomplete metamorphosis; an artificial that imitates the immature or nymphal stage of the insect. Nymph imitations usually require (1) heavy down-eyed extended-shank hooks, (2) absorbent materials, and (3) correct nymphal proportion and coloration.

Occiput
The dorsal posterior of the head; the rear or hind area of the insect head.

Ocelli
The two or three simple eyes of an insect (*ocellus,* singular). For illustration, see *Compound eye.*

Operculate
A cover often in the form of fused nymphal gills; the lid gill or gill shield; a cover (*opercula,* plural).

Osmonde
"A superior quality of iron formerly imported from the Baltic regions, for the manufacture of arrow-heads, fish-hooks, etc." *(OED).* "Ye schall make your hokes of steyl & of osmonde" and "the best Swedish iron" (*An Older Form of the Treatyse of Fysshynge Wyth an Angle* [1883] and *glossary* of same by Thomas Satchell).

Ova
Insect eggs (*ovum,* singular).

Ovipositing
The act of laying or depositing insect eggs.

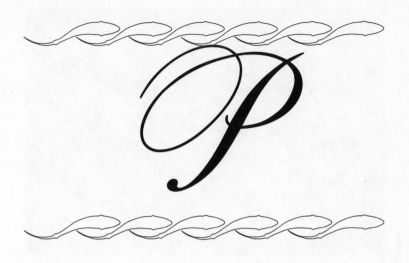

Palmer

A forward-spiraling hackle, a running hackle, with or without stem gaps; also called a *buzz hackle*; any fly tied with a palmer hackle. The tying technique of spiraling a hackle laterally along the shank or body of a fly; the hackled, artificial fly resembling the Palmer-worm, dated 1651; an artificial resembling a Palmer-worm, a hairy, wandering *tineid* moth larva. The term *palmer* comes from the wandering pilgrim-beggar or palmer; ". . . The palmer got its name from the pilgrims who walked . . . to the Holyland in fulfillment of a vow. When they came back home they wore pieces of palm leaves in their hats to signify they had made that long journey and were called palmers. . . . Because a caterpillar, with all its legs, does a lot of walking, it likewise became a palmer" (Harold Smedley, *Fly Patterns and Their Origins* [1950]). The medieval palmer wore crossed palm leaves to indicate his travels. "The Palmer Worm is a small worm covered with hair, supposed to be so called be-

The Palmer Worm pattern. Note that the longer barbs appear at the front of the pattern.

cause it wanders over all plants" (Charles Bowlker, *The Art of Angling* [1839]).

Palps
The small, jointed sensory organs projecting from the maxilla or labia of an insect; an appendage. See *Insect (nomenclature).*

Parachute
The tying technique of horizontal hackling on a vertical stem, such as the wing base. See *Proportions, Parachute Dry Fly* for illustration.

Parachute hook
A fly hook designed to allow the hackle to radiate horizontally, thus supporting the fly body on the water surface. The parachute hook, also known as the "gyro," came from William A. Brush, a Detroit automotive engineer. On April 16, 1931, Brush applied for a patent of a special loop-eye hook for tying parachute dry flies. The

purpose of the patent (#1,973,139, September 11, 1934) was "to provide an artificial fly, in which the hackle is so related to the hook that when the latter is in its properly suspended position, the position of the fly will closely correspond to the position that a live fly would have on the water. . . ." Brush's patent allowed for (1) a return eye-loop to form the hackle extension, (2) a shank-loop hackle extension, and (3) an attached separate hackle extension. Parachute hooks were also produced in England under the name *Ride-Rite,* British patent #379,343. "The hackles of this series of Flies are tied to a projection standing at right angles to the shank of the hook so that the spread of the hackle lies in the same plane as the hook shank and, consequently, is better arranged to support the fly in the correct position on the water" (advertisement, Hardy Brothers of Alnwick, undated). T. R. Henn, in *Practical Fly-Tying* (1950), notes that the "hackle-setting [of the parachute hook] shows up the full values of the body-colour; and many fishermen consider this to be the most important component of the fly." Gerald Burrard, in *Fly-Tying: Principles & Practice* (1945), also notes that

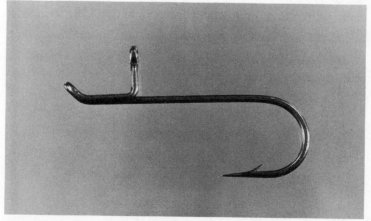

Herter's English Parachute Hook (Number 432). Note the top "eye" on the extension bar that secures the parachute wraps.

Alexander Martin produces parachute patterns with "a small carrier of stout gut or fine wire which sticks out vertically from the middle of the shank of the hook. The result is that the plane of the hackle lies on top of the surface of the water, and the whole effect of the hackle is to ensure the hook floating in a horizontal position."

Paternoster line

A weighted fishing line with hooks attached at intervals, so-called because of the resemblance to a rosary, in which the paternoster bead, "The Lord's Prayer," occurs at intervals. "The Paternoster is simply a gut line, a yard or four feet long, with hooks about a foot apart, and weighted at the end with a bullet or pear-shaped plummet" (Francis Francis, *A Book on Angling* [1876]).

Pattern

A specific artificial fly; a list of the materials and, occasionally, the methods for dressing a particular fly.

Perfect bend

A hook bend characterized by a rounded heel that distributes the stress for optimum mechanical strength; also called the *round bend.* The long bite on a perfect hook provides deep penetration; however, the deep bite and long spear can result in poor strike penetration. Some hook designers, such as Mustad, have adopted a modified perfect bend to reduce the claimed disadvantages. The term origin is prob-

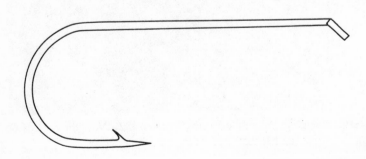

ably based on this design being a solution to the earlier faults found in angular hooks, especially the sneck bend.

Periphyton

The organic slime on submerged objects; the benthic plant system. Dr. C. E. Cushing, a stream ecologist from the Northwest United States, notes that the term *periphyton* technically refers to phyton (plants) and peri (around). The German term *Aufwuchs* may be more accurate, because it includes the detritus, bacteria, algae, and invertebrates that constitute the complete community. "The German term *'Aufwuchs'* has a much broader connotation than the closest English equivalent 'periphyton.' *Aufwuchs* comprises all attached organisms . . . which are usually considered as benthos by American authors. . . " (G. E. Hutchinson, *A Treatise on Limnology,* Volume 1 [1957]).

Periwinkle

The cased or uncased Tricoptera; term probably related to the European intertidal snail with a thick, spiraled, cone-shaped shell; a term from Old English *pinewincle* and Latin *pina,* a mussel.

Pharate

The recently emerged adult still clinging to the pupal husk; the recently hatched adult; said of insects.

Pickled

Speckled, like a hen wing; *"pick"* as a printing term means speck or blotch, 1578 *(OED).* "The head is of black silk or haire, the wings of a feather of a Mallart, Teele or pickled henwing" (John Dennys, *The Secrets of Angling* [1652]).

Photoperiod

The length of daylight; the seasonal length of daylight, said to be a factor in insect emergence.

Phototropism
The response to light. Flora and fauna that avoid light are said to be negatively phototropic.

Plaited
"A contexture of three or more interlaced strands of hair, ribbon, straw etc." *(OED)*; to braid or intertwine, as in a plaited horsehair fly line.

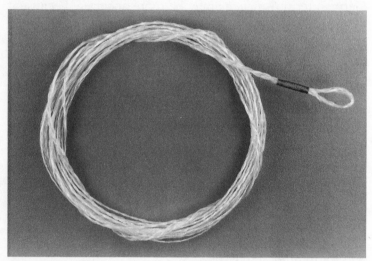

A plaited (woven) horsehair fly line: Staggered strands in decreasing numbers are periodically woven in to create the knotless taper.

Plastron
The air sack or film covering the body during submergence; the air cloak held on by hairs or scales, usually said of water beetles. The air film on the body surface that the insect breathes when submerged.

Play
In angling, "To play a fish, means to humour his violent motions until he becomes exhausted, so that he may not break your line" (J. March, *The Jolly Angler* [1842]).

Plumose

Plume or featherlike; often said of insect antennae or gills.

Points or hackle points

Hackle points or hackle-tip wings. "The Spent Gnat is often dressed with four sharply bright points, of a badger or brownish dun cock's hackle . . ." (G. E. M. Skues, *Silk, Fur and Feather* [1950]).

Posterolateral spines

The spines located on the hind, lateral edge of body segments; said of insects.

Posting

In fly tying, a thread maneuver that consolidates and positions individual, dry-wing bundles. Posting, also called post wrap or base wrap, is especially useful for adjusting

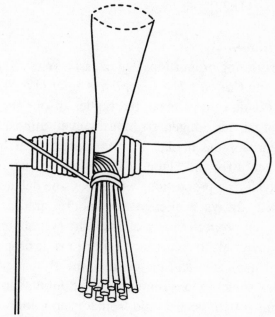

Posting wings

stiff or defiant hair wings. Sometimes three ascending flat wraps are covered by three descending flat wraps to create articulated wings that may be easily adjusted to various positions. After posting, the thread may anchor the bundle into position. If the thread comes from the outside of the wing to anchor as illustrated, then the wing bundles draw together. If the thread comes from between the wings and anchors at the opposite shank side, then the wings are divided and drawn back. The particular wing problem determines the direction of posting and anchoring.

Prime

"Of a fish: To leap or 'rise' " 1787 *(OED)*. "Now and then prime or rise up like a large roach" (Francis Francis, *A Book on Angling* [1876]). "Fishes are said to prime when they leap out of the water" (Thomas Best, *The Art of Angling* [1822]).

Proportions

Proper fly-tying proportions began early. When Viator, in Walton and Cotton's *The Complete Angler* (1766), noted that in London they "make the bodies of our flies both much larger and longer, so long as even almost to the very beard of the hook," Piscator replies that he was given such a fly and "hung it in his parlour window to laugh at." Tying proportions will always be debated, and tyers will always challenge and modify tradition. No matter what proportion is preferred, the tyer should control the materials to create the proportions. If proportions are not established and maintained, the fly pattern may lack that stance and symmetry so admired. However, variations often occur. And some proportions—especially those of the pupa, larva, shrimp, and streamer—offer greater freedom.

Although most proportion precepts emphasize material length, proportions may also include such elements as material quantity, shank location, and mounting stance. Some proportions may not be based on the fly performance or on the natural insect. J. Edson Leonard attempted to provide actual practical function to pattern design when he popularized "the ideal float line" in *Flies* (1960). He depicted the dry fly floating on its tail and hackle tips with the hook barely brushing the surface. Theoretically, the "pendulum" hook bend cocks the wings up, but the tail and hackle proportions prevent the hook from touching the water surface. In actual use, of course, the dry fly quickly penetrates the surface with portions of hook, body, and barbs. So that the wings appear to emerge from the middle of the hackle, dry flies

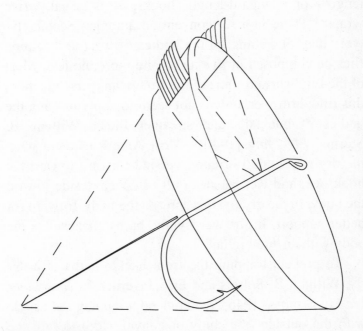

Ideal float line

may have an equal number of hackle turns behind and in front of the wings.

The following proportions are based on traditional concepts. Fly-tying proportions, however, may always vary according to the individual tyer and the region. As Ralph Waldo Emerson once said, "A foolish consistency is the hobgoblin of little minds." The hook shank begins directly behind the hook eye and travels to a point on the shank directly above the rear of the barb. The hook bend usually begins at the end of the rear of the shank and terminates at the beginning of the hook spear. Not all tyers include the head space in the shank length. A slightly longer tail (based on a longer shank length) increases the delicacy of design. Hook length is the distance between the total limits of hook bend and eye. Hook gap (gape) is the distance between the hook point and shank. The number of ribbing wraps depends on ribbing width and hook length—on standard-length hooks, it is usually five wraps. "There is a set convention amongst Scotch fly-tyers that all ribbing on the bodies of trout and salmon flies be composed of *five* turns—no more, no less. Most of the English, and some of the American tyers, adhere to this rule; however, it does not seem to apply in tying the bodies of bucktails and streamer flies" (William B. Sturgis, *Fly-Tying* [1940]). Most American tyers wrap the dry hackle dull or concave side forward toward the hook eye, and wet hackles dull or concave side toward the body. In the dry fly, this spreads the barbs forward for better support. In the wet fly, the barbs encapsulate the body with an "umbrella."

To prevent trapping the front hackle barbs of a dry fly, William B. Sturgis and Eric Taverner, in *New Lines for Fly-Fishers* (1946), recommend wrapping the hackle with the outside (the shiny or convex side) toward the eye. Wrapped in this manner, the barbs bend back, away from the subsequent turns: "Be sure, when the hackle is raised away from the hook preparatory to winding, that the shiny side is facing towards the eye of the hook. Unless this is done it is hard to prevent a few fibres from being folded in." Modern, genetic hackles, especially the smaller sizes, often lack the distinct barb curvature. On such hackles, either side may face forward.

The following drawings illustrate conventional and alternative proportions. In hook orientation, the *front* of the shank is at the eye and the *rear* is at the bend.

Traditional Dry Fly

Tail: Hackle-barb tails equal hook shank or two and one-half hook gap. William B. Sturgis recommended that five or six hackle barbs are usually sufficient. Some tyers select tails slightly proud of the shank length. Dun tails may equal one and one-quarter shank length, and the longer spinner tails may equal one and three-quarters

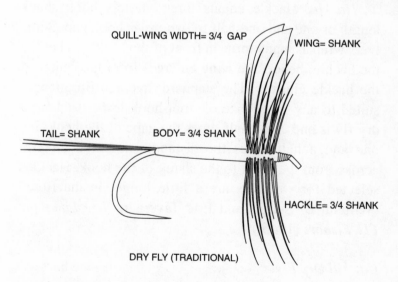

Traditional quill-wing dry fly

shank length. The tail is usually mounted on the shank directly above the rear of the barb. The tail mount point may have derived from tying salmon-fly patterns. Notice that James O'Gorman, when tying salmon patterns, began the tag directly above the barb. ". . . Then opposite the beard of the hook put on the tail, *viz.*: tinsel, gold cord or only silk. . . " (*The Practice of Angling* [Reprint 1993]).

Body: The slightly tapered body begins on the hook shank directly above the rear of the barb and ends behind the wings or hackle. Body length equals three-quarter shank length (Eric Leiser, *The Book of Fly Patterns* [1987]).

Wing: The quill wing length equals hook shank or two times the hook shank. Maximum wing length equals total hook length. Quill wing width may equal three-quarters hook gap. Wing set begins in the front one-fifth or one-quarter of hook shank. Barb and hackle wing equals hook shank.

Hackle: Hackle equals three-quarters hook shank length or one and one-half to two times hook gap. Some tyers wrap as many turns in front of the hackle as behind the hackle; hence, the wing emerges from the center of the hackle cluster. "The standard, average fibre-length suited to any given size of trout-hook to be used for a dry fly is one and a half times the gape of the hook, i.e. one and a half times the distance measured directly across from the point to the shank of the hook. Hackles selected for wet flies are a little longer in the fibre" (William B. Sturgis and Eric Taverner, *New Lines for Fly-Fishers* [1946]).

Catskill Dry Fly
Tail: Sparse tail slightly longer than hook shank.

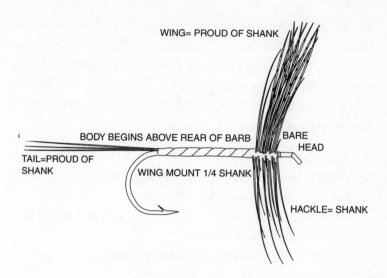

WING= PROUD OF SHANK

BODY BEGINS ABOVE REAR OF BARB

BARE HEAD

TAIL=PROUD OF SHANK

WING MOUNT 1/4 SHANK

HACKLE= SHANK

Catskill dry fly

Body: Body begins on hook shank somewhere above rear of barb and hook point.

Wing: Slightly longer than shank length and sometimes moderately canted forward, mounted one-quarter to one-third shank length behind the eye. (*Note:* Catskill patterns may be tied in traditional dry-fly proportions, i.e., tail and wing may equal shank length.)

Hackle: A few sparse wraps of stiff cock hackle, often blue dun or ginger.

Neck: A distinct, bare neck about one eye length from the hook eye. Minimal thread wraps form a modest head. The bare neck may not appear on modern commercial flies. Originally, the bare neck allowed space for the gut knot. The head is usually sparsely wrapped. Elsie Darbee once said that anything beyond two head wraps is superfluous.

Exactly what the distinctive features of this graceful American style were and who created them is still a controversy. According to Harry Darbee, Roy Steenrod was perhaps the tyer most responsible for passing on the distinctive features of the Catskill style. Darbee inventories those various features:

1. A generous hook, typically a size 12, perfect bend
2. A particularly slender and sparse body, usually spun fur or stripped peacock herl
3. A divided wing, usually made from mottled barbs of a wood duck flank feather
4. A few sparse turns of an extremely stiff, glassy cock hackle, mostly blue dun or ginger
5. The wings and hackle set back from the eye of the hook, leaving "a clean neck at the expense of a slightly shortened body." The hackle moves closer to the balance point of the pattern so that "the fly rides over broken, turbulent waters like a coast guard lifeboat, so nearly balanced that often the tail of hackle whisks (originally a little curlicue of several wood-duck barbules [*sic*]) doesn't touch the water at all" Harry Darbee with Austin Mac Francis, *Catskill Flytier* (1977).

Thorax-Wing Dun (Marinaro)
    Tail: Tail, split at right angles to shank, equals shank length. Casting invariably reduces the angle. Vincent Marinaro used one tail barb per side on hook sizes 22 and 24, two barbs per side on sizes 18 and 22, and three barbs per side on sizes 16 and 14. A turn or two of thread behind the tail barbs and a drop of cement at the base secures the angles.
    Body: No body, only a small thoracic dubbing ball at wing base. The thoracic ball anchors the figure-eight turns of hackle.

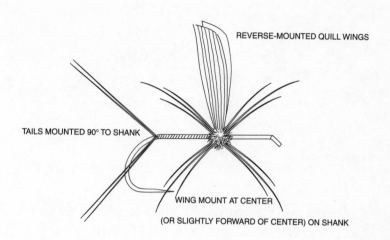

REVERSE-MOUNTED QUILL WINGS

TAILS MOUNTED 90° TO SHANK

WING MOUNT AT CENTER

(OR SLIGHTLY FORWARD OF CENTER) ON SHANK

Thorax-wing dun

Wing: Wings mounted at shank center (Marinaro), or slightly forward. Thoracic wing set may also occur as far forward as one-quarter hook shank. Marinaro reverse-mounted quill wings for greater durability (Vincent Marinaro, *A Modern Dry-Fly Code* [1970]).

Hackle: When mounted, the hackle barbs should cloak the bottom of the hook. Wrap hackle on thoracic ball with three crossing turns (figure-eights).

Compara-Dun (Caucci-Nastasi)

Tail: Stiff hackle barbs tied outrigger, divided by a small dubbing ball.

Body: To support wings, dubbed body continues in front of wings.

Wing: Mount wing one-third shank length behind eye. Hair wing fans or radiates 180 degrees on each side

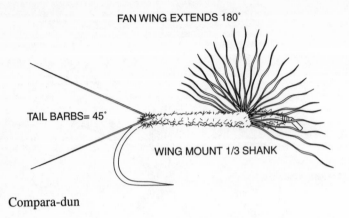

FAN WING EXTENDS 180°

TAIL BARBS= 45°

WING MOUNT 1/3 SHANK

Compara-dun

to support the pattern on the surface of the water (Al Caucci and Bob Nastasi, *Hatches II* [1986]).

Hair-Wing Dry Fly

Tail: Hair or hackle-barb tail equals three-quarters shank length or two times hook gap. Tail may equal the traditional shank length. Some hair-wing patterns have a slightly shorter tail because of the crimped and flared

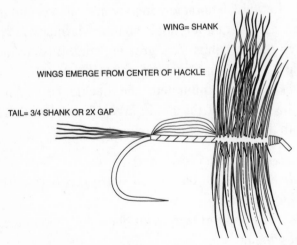

WING= SHANK

WINGS EMERGE FROM CENTER OF HACKLE

TAIL= 3/4 SHANK OR 2X GAP

HACKLE=3/4 SHANK LENGTH AND MAY OCCUPY 1/2 SHANK SPACE

Hair-wing dry fly: the Humpy

fibers intercepting the hypothetical float line earlier than the traditional, straight hackle-barb fibers.

Body: Body begins directly over rear of hook barb and terminates at wing mount point.

Wing: Wing length equals the shank length. Wing mount point may be at the front one-quarter shank length, i.e., the Humpy pattern. There is a unique tying method to the traditional, hair-wing Humpy. Having long, soft hairs for tying makes this pattern much easier to tie. The number of hairs will determine, to a significant extent, the total deer-hair bundle length used in tying the pattern. And the more body hairs that are used, the wider the body bends will be; hence, more length will be required for those bends at the rear and at the wing base. Fewer hairs, of course, bend more abruptly. The length of the deer hair will constitute the underbody, the overbody, and the wings. Therefore, the correct amount and length of the hair bundle are critical.

Hackle: Hackle barb length equals three-quarter shank length. A dry fly hackle (with multiple wraps) may occupy half of the total shank length.

Quill-Wing Wet Fly

Tail: The tail equals one-half shank length, or tail extends to rear extremity of the overwing. The tail should not "exceed a total length of more than twice the gape of the hook, and preferably not more than one and a half" (William B. Sturgis and Eric Taverner, *New Lines for Fly-Fishers* [1946]). On some patterns, tail length may equal shank length.

Body: Body begins directly above the rear of the barb and ends at the rear of the hackle mount point.

Wing: Wing length varies. Wing length may be "just proud of [beyond] the hook bend," equal to the shank length, or one and one-quarter to one and one-half shank

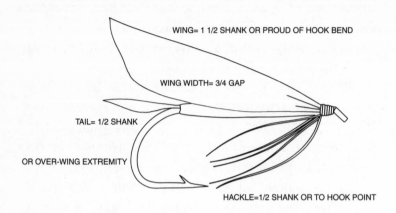

WING= 1 1/2 SHANK OR PROUD OF HOOK BEND

WING WIDTH= 3/4 GAP

TAIL= 1/2 SHANK

OR OVER-WING EXTREMITY

HACKLE=1/2 SHANK OR TO HOOK POINT

Quill-wing wet

length. Wet-fly wing width is approximately three-quarters hook gap. Wing-mount point, slightly beyond a head length from the eye, is forward of the dry-fly wing-mount point. "The length of wings made from slips of web, cut or torn from the primary or from secondary feathers, is in most flies equal to that of the hook" (William B. Sturgis and Eric Taverner, *New Lines for Fly-Fishers* [1946]). The following illustration depicts the so-called *sedge mount* wings that partially enclose the body on each side. Wings may be mounted, after hackling, directly on top of the shank. Although some wet patterns may imitate ovipositing insects with extended wings, William B. Sturgis asserts that "the wings of the wet fly are . . . *immature* and lie closely along the body" (*Fly-Tying* [1940]).

Hackle: The soft-hackle barbs may extend to the hook point, may equal hook gap, or may equal one-half hook-shank length. William B. Sturgis and Eric Taverner, in *New Lines for Fly-Fishers* (1946), recommend that

"Hackles selected for wet flies are a little longer [than 1½ times the hook gap] in the fibre."

Soft-Hackle Fly

Tail: None.

Body: Body lengths variable. Body may imitate the standard hook-shank lengths of dry and wet patterns. Body length may also conform to Scottish tying tradition (W. H. Lawrie, *Scottish Trout Flies* [1966]).

Tweed style: Body ends midway above hook point and hook barb.

Clyde style: Body ends at midshank.

Tummel style: Body ends at front one-quarter shank.

Hackle: The soft-hackle barb length equals the shank length or rear extremity of hook. Often two or three wraps of hackle only.

Thorax: Traditionally none. According to Sylvester Nemes in *The Soft-Hackled Fly* (1975), the addition of the thorax was a later development. If present, the tho-

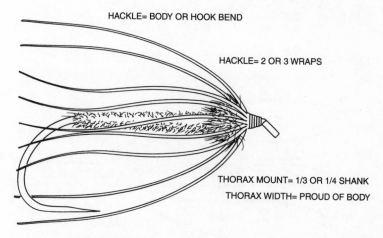

Soft-hackle fly with thorax

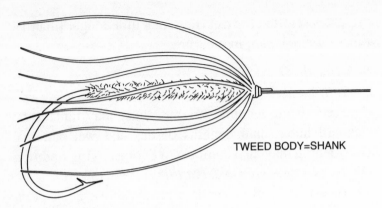

The Tweed style soft-hackle fly

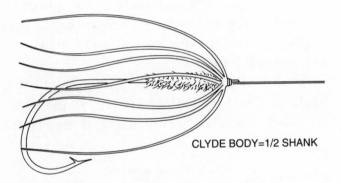

The Clyde style soft-hackle fly

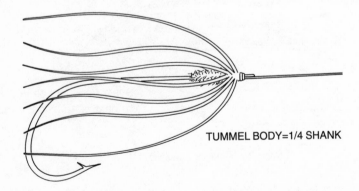

The Tummel style soft-hackle fly

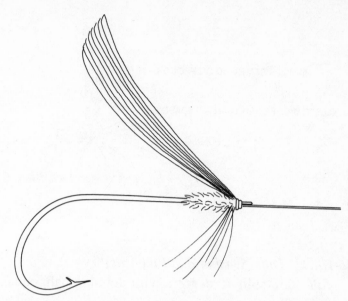

Woodcock and Harelug, an elegant winged Tummel, ca. 1890

racic segment (slightly fuller than the body to encourage the hackle barbs to spread and pulsate during the retrieve) is approximately one-third to one-quarter hook-shank length. Nemes also notes that the term *soft hackle* first appeared in E. M. Tod's *Wet-Fly Fishing* (1914): "The only objection to the soft hackle that I can see, is, that it does not last long. . . ."

Parachute Dry Fly

Tail: Standard, shank length.

Wing: Wing mounting point is one-quarter shank length from hook eye (Dick Talleur, *The Versatile Fly Tyer* [1990]). Wing materials include calf tail, calf body hair, goat hair, and various synthetic yarns.

Hackle: For increased flotation, hackle barbs may be slightly longer than the standard three-quarter hook-shank length. Because of increased flotation of longer, horizontal barbs, some tyers use fewer hackle wraps.

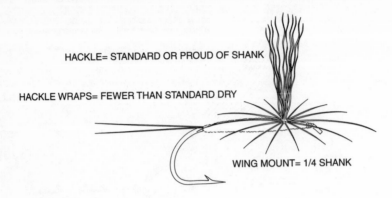

HACKLE= STANDARD OR PROUD OF SHANK

HACKLE WRAPS= FEWER THAN STANDARD DRY

WING MOUNT= 1/4 SHANK

Parachute dry fly

No-Hackle Dun (Swisher and Richards)

Tail: Tail, split 45 degrees with dubbing ball, equals shank length.

Body: Body equals shank length.

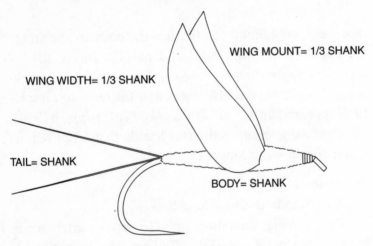

WING MOUNT= 1/3 SHANK

WING WIDTH= 1/3 SHANK

TAIL= SHANK

BODY= SHANK

No-Hackle Dun

Wing: Wing length equals shank length. Wing width equals approximately one-third shank length. Wing mount point equals one-third shank. The lower edge of the wing acts as outrigger (Doug Swisher and Carl Richards, *Selective Trout* [1971]).

Hen-Spinner Dry Fly (Swisher and Richards)

Tail: Tail equals one and one-half shank length. Tail split angle equals 45 degrees.

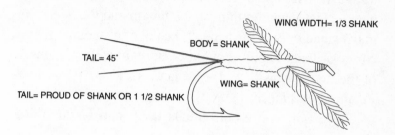

WING WIDTH= 1/3 SHANK
BODY= SHANK
TAIL= 45°
WING= SHANK
TAIL= PROUD OF SHANK OR 1 1/2 SHANK

Hen-Spinner dry fly

Body: Body equals shank length.

Wing: Wing length equals shank length. Wing width equals approximately one-third shank length (Doug Swisher and Carl Richards, *Selective Trout* [1971]).

Streamer

Streamer proportions may vary significantly by tyer and region. Various streamer types encourage different proportions. There are "damp" streamers (muddlers), marabou streamers, bucktail streamers, hackle streamers, miniature

12214.p.113.eps

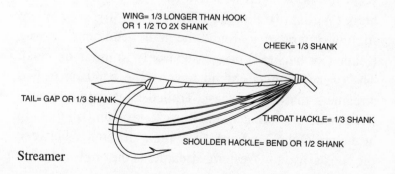

WING= 1/3 LONGER THAN HOOK
OR 1 1/2 TO 2X SHANK
CHEEK= 1/3 SHANK
TAIL= GAP OR 1/3 SHANK
THROAT HACKLE= 1/3 SHANK
SHOULDER HACKLE= BEND OR 1/2 SHANK

Streamer

streamers (dace patterns), pulsating splayed-wing streamers (spruce streamers), and saltwater streamers.
Proportions may be partly based on the aquatic creature or
forage fish imitated. To prevent "short strikes," the tail
may be less than one-third shank length and the overwing
may extend only to the bend. "The tail of a streamer fly on
a regular length hook should be approximately the length
of the hook shank" (A. J. McClane, *McClane's Standard
Fishing Encyclopedia* [1965]).

Tail: Tail, if present, equals hook gap or one-third
shank length.

Body: The body, usually ribbed, equals shank length
and terminates directly above the rear of the barb.
Ribbing turns are variable, depending on shank length
and ribbing width. Ribbing width and number of wraps
are based on the particular hook. Mustad 9575 (forged
Limerick, one-half inch longer than regular) is a standard
streamer hook. Streamer hooks also include Mustad
33957, Mustad 9674, and Thundercreek style Mustad
36620.

Cheek: If present, cheeks, such as jungle-cock eyes,
extend one-third shank from head.

Wing: Wings (such as saddle or schlappen feathers)
are one-third longer than hook length or one and a half
(John Merwin, *Stillwater Trout* [1980]) to two times
longer than shank length. Hair wing should extend beyond the hook bend equal to the gap of the particular
hook (William B. Sturgis, *Fly-Tying* [1940]). To prevent
fouling or wrapping around the hook bend, an overwing
(feather or bucktail) may extend only to the hook bend.
The overwing may extend beyond the bend on trolled
streamers that are not cast. Trolled streamers may also
have an added "stinger" tail hook to pick up fish that nip
at the tail (John Merwin). "The main difference between
the 'Eastern' and 'Western' streamer is the angle at which

the wing is set—the Eastern method dresses the wing low over the body of the fly, while the Western-style streamer wing is set at an approximate 40-degree angle above the body" (A. J. McClane, *McClane's Standard Fishing Encyclopedia* [1965]).

Shoulder hackle: When wrapped, the shoulder hackle points just touch the hook bend or extend one-half shank length. Shoulder hackle may also equal two-thirds over-wing length (John Merwin).

Throat hackle: Throat hackle (beard) equals one and one-half gap (John Merwin) or one-third shank length from the head. On trolling (harling) patterns, the throat hackle may extend to the hook bend or wing extremity.

Larva, Pupa, and Shrimp

Like streamer and nymph proportions, larva, pupa, and shrimp proportions are variable.

Tail: Short tail or gills, approximately equal to hook gap.

Body: Body length may vary depending on the particular hook bend. With a York or round-bend hook, the body generally extends halfway down the bend to take advantage of the circular form.

Wing pad: If present, the wing pad is one-quarter to one-third body length.

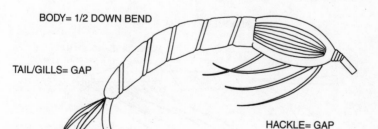

WING PAD= 1/3 TO 1/4 BODY

BODY= 1/2 DOWN BEND

TAIL/GILLS= GAP

HACKLE= GAP

Larva and pupa

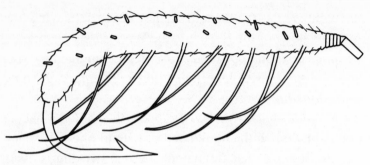

Skues-style Shrimp

Hackle legs: Leg hackle equals hook gap.

Note: Larva and shrimp patterns often vary in proportions depending on the natural and the hook shape. Some tyers use the standard nymph proportions for larva and shrimp. Some tyers also believe that shrimp patterns should be tied on straight-shanked hooks, using one-half of the bend for body curvature. "Body—Seal's fur mixed with pale orange and olive, tied to below the bend of the hook to suggest the curve of the shrimp's back" (G. E. M. Skues, *Side-Lines, Side-Lights & Reflections* [undated]).

Nymph
Nymph proportions may vary, depending on the insect imitated.

Tail: Tail equals one-half hook shank. Stonefly tail equals three-quarters hook shank (William B. Sturgis, *Fly Tying* [1940]).

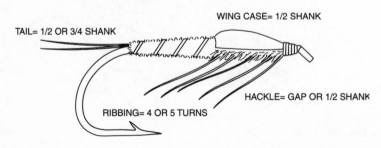

ABDOMEN= 1/2 SHANK

WING CASE= 1/2 SHANK

TAIL= 1/2 OR 3/4 SHANK

HACKLE= GAP OR 1/2 SHANK

RIBBING= 4 OR 5 TURNS

Body: Abdomen equals one-half hook shank. Head and thorax equal one-half hook shank. Head and thorax on natural stonefly and mayfly nymphs equal approximately one-half their total respective body lengths.

Ribbing: Four or five equally spaced turns. Total ribbing wraps depend on shank length, especially extended-shank lengths.

Wing case: Wing case equals thorax (one-half shank length) minus the head space.

Hackle legs: Hackle equals hook gap or one-half hook shank.

Floating Emerger

When tied on standard hooks, floating emergers usually assume the proportions of a dry fly. When tied on circular hooks, floating emergers usually adopt the proportions of a pupa or larva. To support the pattern, the float pod or veiled wings may be one-half shank length. The hackle legs of an emerging dun pattern should be "not more than two-thirds the length of the body" (Doug Swisher and Carl Richards, *Emergers* [1991]). Swisher and Richards also advocated the "shuck" (if present) to be one-half

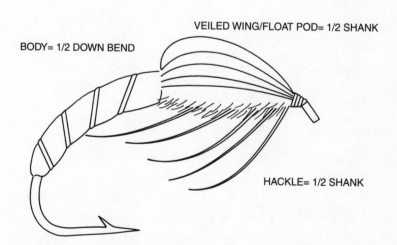

VEILED WING/FLOAT POD= 1/2 SHANK

BODY= 1/2 DOWN BEND

HACKLE= 1/2 SHANK

shank length. This assumes that half of the insect is still attached. Shank-length shucks may also be used.

Proud

A sense of excessiveness, overgrown, hence "beyond," as in a wing "slightly proud of the hook bend."

Puparium

The pupal case of insects; (*puparia,* plural).

Quill

The rachis or stem of a feather or hackle; the barb sections mounted as wings, i.e., the "panel section" of a feather, the quill wing; the stripped herl from the eyed-tail of the peacock. Notice the three basic meanings of quill in fly tying. "By 'quills' one does not in general mean what is ordinarily understood by the term, but single stripped fibers of feathers such as those from the eye or the side of the peacock feather, or from the pinion of a condor" (G. E. M. Skues, *Silk, Fur and Feather* [1950]). A stripped peacock herl. ". . . The herl down each side of the [peacock] feather gives, when stripped of its flue, a good strong brown quill" (Roger Woolley, *Modern Trout Fly Dressing* [1932]). See *Feather (nomenclature).* The term quill also includes a stripped hackle or herl wrapped as a fly body as well as a porcupine quill. At the turn of the century, large feathers, such as condor feathers, were also called "quills."

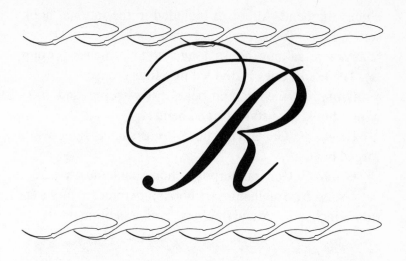

Rachis

The central shaft of a feather; the vane stem.

Raffia

Raffia grass. Also rafia, raphia, or rofia (Frederic M. Halford). A Malagasy word for the palm of the genus *Raphia.* The stripped, soft fiber is sometimes used for tying, especially for the mayfly body.

Rank

"Hooks are denominated rank, when the point and barb project much" (J. March, *The Jolly Angler* [c. 1842]).

Rational hook (hook design)

Because of the ambiguous and confused system of hook notations, T. E. Pryce-Tannatt, in *How to Dress Salmon Flies* (1914), advocated and designed a "rational" hook notation. With the exception of small summer hooks (Group D), "the increment of variation is ¼ inch (which is quite small enough for all practical purposes in general salmon fishing. . . ." The "over-all" measurement includes the bend. Although included in the rational hook series, Pryce-Tannatt rejected eyed hooks (Group D) and heavy-wire salmon hooks longer than 2 inches (Group A). The hook series is divided into four groups:

Group A: General purpose, early-spring and late-winter hook, Dee style, forged bend

Group B: General purpose, long shank, light wire, forged bend

Group C: General purpose, short shank, heavy wire

Group D: Small summer hooks, increments of variation ⅛ inch, singles and doubles, eyed and blind

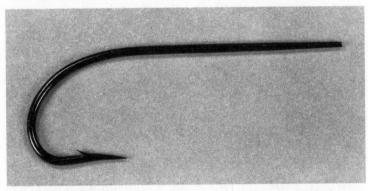

T. E. Pryce-Tannatt's general-purpose, sproat, short-shank, heavy-wire rational hook

Realism
See *Imitation.*

Rectrices
The tail feathers that direct the flight, 1768 *(OED)*. The large, stiff, asymmetrical pennaceous feathers along the posterior edges of the tail. See *Remiges.*

Remiges
The primary and secondary wing feathers that, with the rectrices, comprise most of the airfoil for flying; the large flight feathers along the posterior edge of the wing. Pri-

mary remiges differ from secondary remiges in being more pointed, more stiff, and, usually, more asymmetrical. Both the rectrices and the remiges include the largest feathers of a flying bird.

Reverse wing

In fly tying, an early method of mounting a wing and then reversing or folding it back over the body.

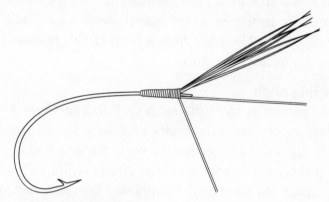

Mount wing with tips forward.

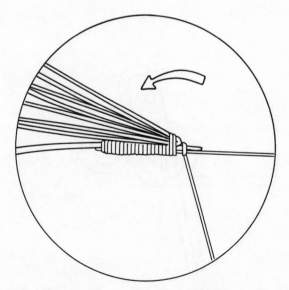

Fold wings back and secure with minimal thread overwraps.

Rheophilic
Associated with currents or flowing water. See *Rheotropism.*

Rheotropism
The response to current flow; a trout that must keep its head upstream is said to possess positive rheotropism. A more accurate term might be *rheotaxis—rheo* (current) and *taxis* (arrangement or orientation); the term *tropism* is usually restricted to botanical phenomena. Cecil E. Heacox's *The Compleat Brown Trout* (1974) popularized the various tropisms of trout.

Riffling hitch
Also known as the *riffle hitch* or *Portland Creek hitch* (place of origin); a secondary knot so designed that the fly scrapes or riffles across the water surface. It may also be tied to sunken patterns for an erratic swim. To hitch a fly, attach the fly with the customary knot and then take one or two half-hitches with the tippet or leader on the

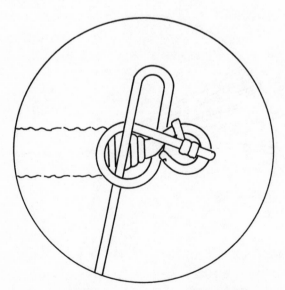

Place one or two half-hitches over the head and tighten.

head immediately behind the hook eye. The tippet or leader stands at a right angle to the hook shank. Lee Wulff popularized the riffling hitch. Originally, local anglers on Portland Creek in northwestern Newfoundland used the riffling hitch to increase the security of knots made from old gut. The result was a pattern that riffles or scrapes the water to attract fish. The tippet comes off the pattern at a particular angle. If the river flows to the left, the tippet should extend from the left side of the head (viewed from above with the head pointed away). If the river flows to the right, the tippet should extend from the right side of the head. Half-hitches may slightly weaken nylon line. The riffling hitch may be effective for any aggressive game fish, including trout and bass.

Riparian
Associated with the bank or margin of stream or river; the inhabitants, the flora or fauna, of the bankside.

Rogan wing hold
When mounting quill wings on handheld salmon patterns, the Michael Rogan hold supports the wings on both sides while the thread is pulled taut. Rogan's original hold used the right thumb and the left index finger to secure the wings. Using the right index finger instead of the right thumb seems more natural. The thumb and index fingers of the left hand grip the hook and wing. Make one soft thread loop over the wing. Then with the middle finger of the left hand and the index finger of the right hand, hold the wing in front of the thread wrap. With the thumb and middle finger of the right hand, pull the thread down to secure the wing. Make additional wraps over the wing base to "confirm" the mount. This method, which encourages flat, vertical wings, supports the wings on both sides during the downward, tightening thread pressure. Although originally created for hand-

tying, the method also works when using a vise. In *How to Dress Salmon Flies* (1914), T. E. Pryce-Tannatt describes a similar thumb-finger hold. Pryce-Tannatt used his method to mount curved "strip" tail fibers on salmon patterns.

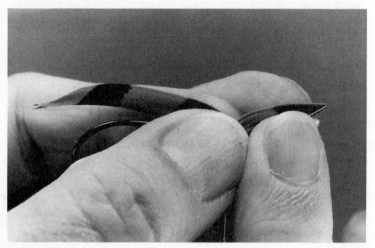

Notice that the fingers support the wing behind and in front of the thread wraps. The thread, which will be pulled down, may be seen between the fingers.

Rolled wings

Usually a roll or bundle of wing or tail barbs mounted erect (like mayfly wings), or down (like caddis wings), either single or divided.

S-twist

S-twist indicates the direction of the twist of tying threads. The middle line (or diagonal) of the letter "S" indicates the twist direction. See *Z-twist*.

Sad

"Of colour: Dark, deep, Late Medieval" and "Dark-coloured, sober-coloured" 1711 *(OED)*. "Bears Hair of diverse Colours . . . Gray, Dun, light Coloured, *sad* Coloured and bright shining Bears Hair . . ." (James Chetham, *The Angler's Vade Mecum* [1700]).

Saddle feather

The elongated and tapered saddle hackles (the dorsopelvic tract feathers) are upper tail coverts. And, as they are designed to droop, the stems are thin and soft. They are used for large dry-fly hackles, palmer hackles, and salmon and streamer wings. The barbs, although usually as stiff and straight as the spade hackle, often serve as dry-fly tails. Technically, the term *saddle* applies only to the dorsopelvic feathers of the male; the dorsopelvic feathers of the female form a soft back slope and are collectively called the *cushion.*

Salmon fly (nomenclature)

Salmon fly nomenclature is variable. Past and present writers often tangle the terms for side and cheek feathers or call one of them shoulder feathers. Perhaps the most universal approach appears in T. E. Pryce-Tannatt's *How to Dress Salmon Flies* (1914). The traditional fully dressed salmon fly, such as a Jock Scott, has a built-wing and jointed floss body. Much of the grace of a salmon fly lies in the body and wing work. The wing structure may consist of three sections (strip, upper wing, and underwing) covered by three feathers (overwing, side, and cheek). Sometimes the overwing is omitted, and sometimes the wing widths are regular (main wing is one-half hook gap, outer wing is one-half main wing width, and the roof or upper wing is one-half the width of the outer wing. All feathers must have the correct arc and length. The soft, "sheathy" feathers and fibers should allow the various undercolors to show through. All references to T. E. Pryce-Tannatt in this entry are from *How to Dress Salmon Flies* (1914).

Composite Salmon-Fly Nomenclature

1. *Tag* is the first dressed section, which consists of two or three turns directly above the barb. The tag may be divided into two sections such as "silver twist and light blue silk" or "gold twist and light orange silk." The second section of the tag, which has been called the *tip,* is equal to the length of the barb and directly above the barb. Tag materials include tinsel, wire, wool, fur, or floss.
2. *Tail* length is usually one and one-half hook gap. Tail materials include golden pheasant crest, Indian

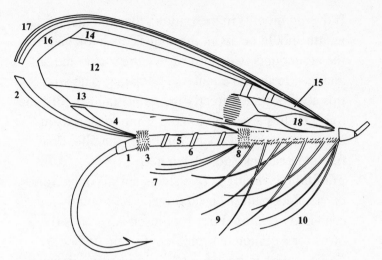

Fully-Dressed Salmon Fly

crow, blue chatterer, blue kingfisher, teal, or wood duck. Other feathers may be combined with the tail, such as golden pheasant tippet, red breast feather, cock of the rock, and red ibis.

3. *Butt* is three or four wraps, depending on the particular pattern. Butt materials include ostrich or peacock herl, yarn, or dubbing.

4. *Tail topping* (sometimes called *tag*) is one-half tail length. Compound tails have "either a feather laid above the topping or tied on each side of the topping, forming thereby cheeks to the tail" (Eric Taverner, *Fly-Tying for Salmon* [1942]). Tail toppings may be hackle, floss, herls, or complete feathers.

5. *Body length* is dependent on style:
   1. Standard length—the tag is directly above the barb
   2. Low-water length—the tag mounts at midshank
   3. Extended low-water length—the tag mounts two-thirds down the shank from the hook eye.

If the tag mounts in the middle, the tail and hackle length should be about three-quarters hook gap. If the tag mounts two-thirds down the shank, the tail and hackle should equal one hook gap. The wing tips always stand directly inside the tail tip. Silk and tinsel bodies are often jointed. Body materials include flat and oval tinsel, dubbing, chenille, floss, fur, and peacock and ostrich herl.

6. Traditional *ribbing* is five shank spirals only. Some of the older patterns used three to four spirals for each body section. Poul Jorgensen advocates five turns for a complete shank length, and on bodies broken up by butts, from two to five turns, depending on the body-section length. Jorgensen also suggests a possible rationale for five turns. "If there were more than five turns of tinsel, the hackle would be too dense and thus adversely affect the performance of the fly" (Poul Jorgensen, *Salmon Flies* [1978]). "In flies ribbed with flat tinsel and possessing a body hackle, twist is used as well, and is wound behind the tinsel as a protection to the hackle" (T. E. Pryce-Tannatt, *How to Dress Salmon Flies* [1914]).

7. *Trailers* or *joint trailers* usually equal the length between the joints. Also called *veiling*. Materials: Indian crow, toucan breast feathers, or floss.

8. The *joint* occurs directly at midshank point. Joints may also occur anywhere on the shank. Materials: Same as butt.

9. *Palmered hackle* length at mount point equals hook gap. Materials: Various wet hackles. Also called *body* or *ribbing hackle*. Throat hackles may be totally different from the palmered hackle. Pryce-Tannatt regards the tail coverts as an exception, both in character and mounting manner.

10. *Throat* or *beard* should be slightly longer than the front hackle barbs, or one and one-half the particular hook gap. Materials: Body hackles from teal, jay, and guinea fowl.

11. *Head* space equals the eye of that particular hook.

12. *Main wing* is slightly short of the tail tip, and the width should be about one-half hook gap. Materials: Various natural or dyed, strip, or married feathers. Pryce-Tannatt classifies salmon flies according to their wings: ordinary or simple strip wings, whole feather wings, mixed wings, built wings, topping wings, and herl wings.

13. *Underwing* matches the length and the taper of the main wing. The underwing is often made up of tippet strands, turkey sections, or jungle cock feathers.

14. *Upper wing strip* or *roof* matches the main wing length and is "normally half the width of the outer wing unless otherwise specified." (Paul Jorgensen). On some patterns, an outer wing sits on the outside and in the middle of the main wing. The outer wing is half the width of the main wing. Upper wing materials include brown mallard shoulder or bronze mallard.

15. *Side feather,* located on the outside of the main wing, is usually one-third to one-half the main wing length and other feathers, often longer. Sometimes called a *shoulder feather.* Pryce-Tannatt notes that the side feather may extend as far back as the butt. Side feathers include jungle cock, starling, teal, or black-barred wood duck.

16. *Topping,* which follows the outer perimeter, joins or not with the tail tip. According to Pryce-Tannatt, the topping is invariably from the golden pheasant's crest and creates "a glistening transparency to the upper edge of the wings," while keeping them together.

17. *Horns,* if present, normally extend to the end of the
wing. Traditionally, single strands of the tail feather
of the macaw are used. Pryce-Tannatt notes that
horns "constitute an element of mobility in a fly,
and mechanically are useful in protecting brittle,
delicate feathers, such as jungle cock, when the latter are used as cheeks or sides."

18. The *cheek* is usually one-half to one gap-width in
length unless otherwise stated (Paul Jorgensen). It
sits on the outside of the side feather:
". . . Cheeks, that is, the last pair of feathers put on
close to the head" (Eric Taverner, *Fly-Tying for
Salmon* [1942]). Sometimes also called *side* or
shoulder feather. Cheek feathers include Indian
crow, blue chatterer, or jungle cock. Pryce-Tannatt
adds that on some patterns, such as the Akroyd, the
cheeks are droop mounted.

Salmon fly (types)

There are several types (classifications) of salmon-fly
patterns, based on proportions, materials, methods, and
angling conditions. The traditional fly types, primarily
based on wing classifications, include the (1) Built Wing,
(2) Mixed Wing, (3) Whole-Feather Wing, (4) Simple-
Strip Wing, (5) Herl Wing, (6) Topping Wing, (7) Dee,
(8) Spey, (9) Grub, and (10) Low Water. Other types of
salmon flies, not included here, are the hair-wings, tube
flies, dry flies, and Irish flies. Pryce-Tannatt defines Irish
flies as "general patterns, possessing as a rule rather
more wing and more variety of colour in the wing. . . .
They have a very common feature in the shape of the
Mallard strips partly veiling the mixed-wing underneath,
and very few of them have the adornment of a topping
over the wing." All excerpts and descriptions are from
Pryce-Tannatt's *How to Dress Salmon Flies* (1914). All

illustrated patterns were tied by tying historian Marvin Nolte.

Built-Wing Salmon Fly: *The Butcher:* married wing and seal body.

"These have as a foundation either a plain wing of paired upright strips or a whole-feather wing. Over this 'married' fibres of several sorts of feathers are imposed in batches of two or more."

Mixed-Wing Salmon Fly: *The Gordon:* married wing and floss body.

"Mixed wings . . . are made up of a number of single strands of various feathers 'married' to each other in one continuous 'sheath.' " "Strictly speaking, a mixed-wing is composed of a number of single strips of several different kinds of feather. Not uncommonly these are tied on in as a bunch anyhow, but usually all the fibres are carefully 'married' one to another in a certain definite order. The appearance of a carefully mixed wing gives one the impression of a Persian carpet, a conglomeration of a multitude of colours. A built-wing, on the other hand, is constructed on bolder lines, and the essential thing about it is, that instead of being tied on all at once, it is built in stages, one portion above another, but in such a manner that, like the tiles of a roof, the portions underneath are left exposed by those immediately above them. Very often the first portion is made up of broad paired strips of some plain feather . . . over which 'married' strips of different feathers are built, but always in such a way as to leave a portion of the first pair visible."

Whole-Feather Wing Salmon Fly: *The Durham Ranger:* tippet and jungle cock wing.

Whole feather wings "are composed of entire feathers (e.g., Golden Pheasant tippet and sword feather, Jun-

gle Cock neck) set on upright in pairs, back to back."
Back to back means "the direct opposition of the under or
inner surfaces, i.e., the outer or 'best' surfaces showing
on each side."

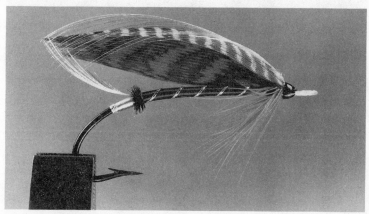

Simple Strip-Wing Salmon Fly: *The Blue Charm:* turkey wing
with teal roof.

"These may be set on (a) with an upright inclination,
or (b) more or less on a slant. The kind of feather used as
well as the manner in which it is put on will influence the
set of this variety of wing."

Herl-Wing Salmon Fly: *The Beauly Snow Fly:* peacock herl strand
wings.

Herl wings "are composed of strands or strips from
either the tail or the sword feathers of the Peacock."

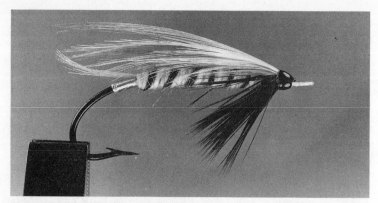

Topping-Wing Salmon Fly: *The Variegated Sun Fly:* tricolor body and six wing toppings.

"Golden Pheasant crest feathers entirely form the wing."

Dee Strip-Wing Salmon Fly: *The Akroyd:* white turkey tail strip wings.

". . . A very distinct group, being peculiar in their appearance and geographical application. They originate from . . . the Aberdeenshire Dee, and are the oldest types of patterns still surviving." According to Pryce-Tannatt, these are large, early-spring or late-winter patterns with sparse dressing and somber colors. They possess "the extreme mobility of hackles and wings, which impart a very life-like appearance to the fly as it works in the water."

Spey Salmon Fly: *The Purple King:* bronze mallard wings, spey hackle and three ribs (one counterwrapped).

"The bodies are short, and have no adornments in the shape of tag, tail or butt; and are usually composed of crewels or Berlin wools of various and varying colors, put on as sparingly as possible. The ribbing tinsel is individually broad and collectively plentiful, and, as often as not, besides thread and twist, gold and silver tinsel are used on one and the same body. The hackles are long and very mobile. Both grey and black Heron hackles are used, but the hackles of a typical Spey fly are obtained from the lateral tail feathers of a certain breed of domestic fowl, known as a 'Spey-cock.' [Tyer misnomer]. The method of putting them on is contrary to the general rule, as they are tied in base first instead of tip first—i.e., the longest fibres are at the tail end of the fly—and they are sometimes wound round the body in the reverse way to the tinsel, a piece of twist or fine oval tinsel being used wound on last over the hackle, to prevent it from getting torn by the fishes' teeth. As a matter of fact, the direction

in which the hackle is wound will depend upon which
side of it is stripped, for only one side is used, and accordingly it may go with or against the body tinsel. . . ."

The Grub Fly: *The Tippet Grub:* tippets wound as hackles

"These are merely glorified palmers, glorified in the
sense that they are as a rule much larger and almost invariably more ornamented than the trouting editions."
According to Pryce-Tannatt, grubs are used in warm
weather and resemble, though remotely, the "caterpillars
prevalent in summer and early autumn."

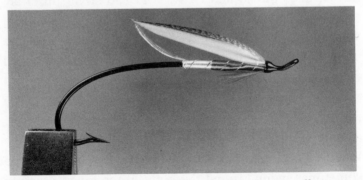

Small Summer Pattern (Low Water): *The Logie:* yellow swan
strips slightly covered by brown mallard strips.

"These are . . . in the main small editions of the regular salmon flies. They are very often dressed on small

double hooks, and the materials are sparingly used."
Pryce-Tannatt concludes that they are late-spring, summer, and early-autumn patterns when settled weather and
clear low water are present.

Schlappen hackle

A long, webby hackle about 24 centimeters long with a
fine diameter stem (about 0.012 inch) used for the De-
Feo-style beards, Spey hackles, and streamer wings. Chi-
nese schlappen are usually strung and often dyed; the
term *schlappen* comes from the German word meaning
"to dangle or to hang loosely"; the all-web or nearly all-
web hackle found between the bird's saddle and the tail
feathers. See *DeFeo style.*

Scissors

Scissors for fly tying may be highly specialized. They
should be short for manipulation with finely tapered
points for close cutting. Large or adjustable open finger-
loops enhance comfort. Blades touch at only two points:
the pivot point and the cut point. The cut point moves
along the edges of the shear bars as both blades "wrap"
around each other while closing. Thus a single shear
point passes down the edges when the scissors close.

Scissors have two blades: the guillotine (the moving
blade) and the anvil (the stationary blade). The blade connected to the thumb is the guillotine. The other blade is
the anvil. The thumb presses down on the guillotine blade
to cut. Most blades score about one to one and one-half
points on the Rockwell C scale. A greater differential between blade hardness may cause one blade to attack the
other. The blade angles are approximately the same.
Many tyers taper the tips for fine cutting. When tapering
the tips with a file, do not wipe too much metal off the
back of the tips, because this lessens the cross-section and
decreases the closing pressure. Blades with microserra-
tions are recommended for cutting resistant materials,

such as the slick synthetics and deer hair. For optimal effi-
ciency, the serrations should be located on the stationary
anvil blade. Serrations on the moving guillotine are less
likely to capture material. The edge bevel is usually about
25 to 30 degrees, but scissors designed for special materials may be beveled to 40 degrees. Both the anvil and guillotine blades may have the same edge bevel.

Scissors are either right- or left-handed. Right-handed
scissors slightly orbit the top finger-loop to the left,
thereby increasing pressure at the shear point. Right-
handed scissors used in the left hand orbit the top finger-
loop to the right, thereby decreasing the pressure at the
shear point. Scissors used in this manner may not cut
well, especially with a slack pivot screw or wear.

During tying, scissors may be kept or worn in the
hand. Place the ring finger through the lower loop and nes-
tle the top loop in the palm. The scissors can be rotated beneath the wrist, where the small finger controls them when
not in use. If the index finger lowers the finger-loop, then
the forefinger is free for tying. When cutting, merely rotate
the scissors into the hand and cradle it in the natural fold
formed by the forefinger and thumb. The thumb is then
placed on or in the upper loop for cutting. After cutting, the
scissors again rotate beneath the hand while the tying continues. Wearing scissors may seem awkward at first, but in
time they will become an extension of the hand and their
use will increase. A single blade edge can closely slice a
thread, or a fine point can rough thoracic dubbing.

Tying Scissors Features

1. Finely tapered, sharp points (A 15-degree tapered
   point is best for fine, close cutting.)
2. Large comfortable or adjustable finger loops
3. Well-meshing blades with a smooth shear action
4. An adjustable pivot screw
5. Points that register or match correctly when closed

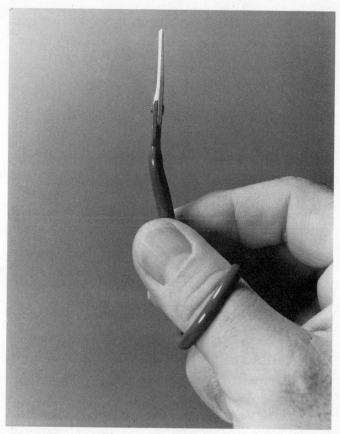

Double offset scissors offer increased tying visibility and close trimming. Note that the finger rings are turned to comfortably cross the thumb and fingers.

6. Serrated edge or edges for synthetic and hair work
7. Magnetic tips for selecting small hooks
8. Uniform angle and width to the cutting bevel

Double offset scissors, a specialized fly-tying design, have canted blades that allow cutting and trimming not possible with conventional tying scissors. The handles are offset and dropped about 35 degrees for complete cutting visibility; neither the hand nor the scissors obscure the cutting. They are especially appropriate for close cutting and for trimming dubbing loops. The hand and the han-

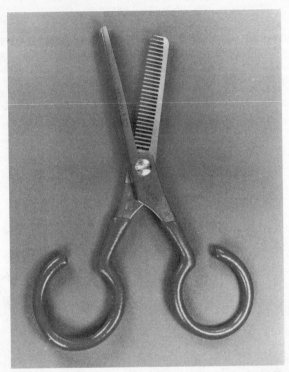

The Taperizer's toothed blades allow thinning, blending, and tapering of strand materials, especially synthetic strand materials on saltwater patterns.

dles avoid the cutting path, so material trapped in a dubbing loop is neither displaced nor dislodged during trimming. The offset blades allow close cropping of fur and hair patches. They have one serrated blade, a functional pivot screw, and adjustable handles. Offset scissors and Taperizers are made by Anvil Industries.

Sclerite
The chitinous body plates of the insect exoskeleton connected by the flexible sutures.

Sclerotized
The hard insect body plates or sclerites.

Scoured

"To cleanse (worms, fish, etc.) by purging, late ME" *(OED)*. "On the bend of the hook put two or three maggots, or a well-scoured worm" (Charles Bowlker, *The Art of Angling* [1839]).

Scut

"A short, erect tail, especially that of a hare, rabbit or deer," 1530 *(OED)*. "Body, black Rabbit's scut" (Izaak Walton, *The Complete Angler* [1766]).

Scutum

The middle section or segment of the insect thoracic notum.

Sessile

Rooted, stalked, or fixed in place.

Seston

The suspended matter, including both flora and fauna, in water.

Seta

Bristlelike; a bristle, often said of insect body hair; (*setae,* plural).

Sheath

In a salmon-fly pattern, the married fibers that constitute a single wing.

Shoulder

The front of the artificial fly body; that part of the artificial fly body immediately behind the wings. "Then wind the silk dubbed with fur round the hook to the shoulder, leaving ample room for the wing and hackle" (G. E. M. Skues, *Silk, Fur and Feather* [1950]).

Shoulder hackle

The front hackle of an artificial fly. According to William F. Blades, the salmon-fly dresser calls the forward hackle a shoulder hackle and the palmer hackle a body hackle. When two hackles are mounted at the shoulder, only the aft-hackle is termed shoulder hackle. "When two hackles are thus wound on, the one nearest the tail is called the 'shoulder hackle' and the forward one is the head hackle" (Gerald Burrard, *Fly-Tying: Principles & Practice* [1945]). The beard hackle of a salmon fly is called a "shoulder hackle" (William B. Sturgis, *Fly-Tying* [1940]), or a "throat hackle" (T. E. Pryce-Tannatt, *How to Dress Salmon Flies* [1914]).

Sickle feather

The cock tail feathers (the rectrices) and the upper major tail coverts form, respectively, the greater and lesser sickle feathers. The sickles serve as streamer wings and, sometimes, Spey hackles. The term *sickle* is derived from the crescent or sickle-blade droop of the feather.

Silk line designations

Silk line diameters, given in inch decimals, are alphabetically designated as follows:

Size	Diameter (Inch)
A	0.060 (larger diameter)
B	0.055
C	0.050
D	0.045
E	0.040
F	0.035
G	0.030
H	0.025
I	0.020 (smaller diameter)

Level lines—those without tapers—have a single-letter designation, such as H. Single tapers have a double-letter designation, such as HD, and double-tapered lines have a triple-letter designation, such as HDH. The specific gravity of silk lines—braided silk impregnated with linseed oil—varied little. With the advent of the synthetic lines—polyvinyl chloride finishes over nylon or Dacron cores—lines varied significantly in weight and consequently required new designations. For general information, split-bamboo specifications follow. Line match depends on the rod construction and the caster. See also *AFTMA line designations.*

Comparative Silk Fly-Line Designations

Line	Double Taper	Weight Forward Taper
DT5F	HEH	HEG
DT6F	HDH	HDG
DT7F	HCH	HCF
WF8F	GBG	GBF
WF9F	GAG	GAF

Simple eyes
The ocelli of an insect. See *Ocelli.*

Skirting fly
"A skirting fly is one which throws off a V-shaped wave when worked on the surface" (G. W. Maunsell, *The Fisherman's Vade Mecum* [1952]).

Slight [sleight, *cf.* sly]
Skill or dexterity; wisdom or knowledge; craft or cunning *(OED).* "You must change his colour [the Waterflie] every Moneth, beginning with a darke white, and so grow to a yellow, the forme cannot so well be put on paper, as it may be taught by slight" (John Dennys, *The Secrets of Angling* [1652]).

Slink, slunk

An abortive or prematurely born animal, particularly a calf. "Of animals, especially cows: To bring forth (young) prematurely or abortively, 1640" *(OED)*. The hair of such an animal used in fly tying. "Dubbing of Castling ["Castling: The offspring of an untimely birth; an abortion—1704" *(OED)*]; "Skins of Calves and colts, that are tewed ["taw: to soften (hides) by beating" *(OED)*]; and several colours and shades of one skin: so of Cushions made of such Skins that have been neatly Tewed in the Skinners Lime-pit: so of Abortive Skins of Colts and Calves, at Skinners Lime-pits Tewed, &c." (James Chetham, *The Angler's Vade Mecum* [1700]).

Smut

The term refers to a variety of small insects, especially the reed smut or black fly *(Simulium spp.)*. The early English origin of the term is related to smudge and soot, a small black particle, perhaps related to Gaelic *smuid,* smoke, and Early Irish *smut,* a cloud. The term has been used in trouting since 1889 (the trout rise to a small insect) and 1899 (a minute black insect) *(OED)*. The smutting rise, a slowly expanding ring with minimal water disturbance. See *Midge. Smutting fish:* When fish are "feeding on very small, black, smutting-looking flies, when they usually refuse the artificial fly altogether" (John Bickerdyke, *The Book of the All-Round Angler* [ca. 1899]).

Sneck

In hook design, a term with multiple meanings: (1) Sometimes used to designate an outpoint or offset (see *Kirby*) opposite to the "reverse" offset; (2) Also refers to a specific, square hook bend; (3) Can also refer to both the offset and the bend—hence, sneck may designate a *square bend,* an *offset spear,* or both.

The origin of the term is obscure, perhaps relating to the Scottish and Northern dialect term *sneck,* the L-shaped latch or catch of a door or gate, or the angular shape of a door catch. The Middle English *snecchen,* with derivative *snekkle,* means "the latch of a door." Perhaps, as Eric Partridge indicates in *Origins* (1983), the term comes "from the 'snap' or click it makes." *Snekkle* also implies the action of catching or "fastening" like a hook.

Sometimes a distinction is made between *sneck* and *snecked,* with the latter referring only to the offset spear. George Leonard Herter, in *Professional Fly Tying, Spinning and Tackle Making* (1971), cautions against confusing the word sneck with snecked. "The word 'sneck' means a specific hook pattern whereas 'snecked' means the spear of the hook offset to the left." Herter makes a similar distinction between kirby (hook pattern) and kirbed (hook spear bent to the right). Herter contends that sneck means the same as *reversed, reversed bend, offset,* or *side bend.* He lists the faults (of dubious accuracy) of all hooks with bent-off spears:

1. It is hard to make the hook penetrate.
2. Fish sense the hook more.
3. It is impossible to hook a fish when it strikes opposite the spear side.
4. Flies often spin when they are trolled.

A *snecked hook* may be one that is square bent *and* kirbed or turned out. In *The Fly Dressers' Guide* (1972), John Veniard defines the sneck trout hook as "a hook with an angular bend and a slight sneck." He also notes that "the outpoint of a 'sneck' hook turns to the right, holding the eye of the hook towards you, while the outpoint of 'reversed' hooks turns to the left." According to Eric Taverner, in *Fly-Tying for Salmon* (1942), "Kirby hooks are snecked, but the peculiar bends given to these marks them off very clearly from pure snecks." G. W.

Maunsell, in *The Fisherman's Vade Mecum* (1952), understood *snecked* as a "bent-off" hook. He even noted that the hook should be *bent off* at the rear or base of the spear, rather than at the top of the bend (shank end). Francis Francis, in *A Book on Angling* (1876), uses *sneck* as an offset point: The hook will "come out without a scratch. Not so if it be slightly twisted, as in the sneck bend."

The square-bend sneck allows the longest possible straight shank length, i.e., the shank length being equal to the hook length. Snecked hooks, such as the once-popular Bartlett's B7362 sneck, were used for dry as well as wet patterns. However, the abrupt angle (which concentrates the mechanical stress) between the shank and the bend was the weakest point. The bend would sometimes break, and the shape eventually fell into disfavor. Although G. E. M. Skues apparently used some sneck bends for his nymphs, he notes in *Minor Tactics of the Chalk Stream* (1910) that "sneck bends of any kind and upturned eyes are deprecated." He preferred, in order, "down-eyed hooks, round, unsnecked, square-bend, and Limerick." Notice here that the terms "unsnecked" and "square-bend" are not synonymous. See *Hook (nomenclature)* for drawings.

Sniggling, snigling, [to] sniggle

The practice of "fishing for eels by means of a baited hook or needle thrust into their holes and haunts," 1661 *(OED)*; from *snig*, a term of unknown origin that first appeared in 1483 and means "a young or small eel" *(OED)*. Any means of taking eels, small or large, is called sniggling. ". . . When the water is lowest, [you] may take a strong, small hook tied to a strong line, or to a string about a yard long, and then into one of these holes . . . or any place where you think an Eel may hide or shelter herself, you may with the help of a short stick put in your bait . . . the Eel will bite instantly, and as certainly gorge it . . . and so get him out by degrees, not pulling too hard" (Izaak Walton, *The Complete Angler* [1766]).

Snood
A length of furled line or wire line; a dropper line. "A hair or catgut line attaching the hook to the rod line (1823)" *(OED)*. Used also as a verb, "To attach (a hook) to a snood (1840)" *(OED)*. "The twisting engine is a useful little appliance for twisting gut and hair into snoods. . . " (John Bickerdyke, *The Book of the All-Round Angler* [ca. 1899]).

Soft-hackled fly
American term for a spider pattern. See *Spider.*

Soft-loop
A common thread maneuver in fly tying. The soft-loop mounts tying material at any given point on a hook. With lateral pressure on the pinch, the thumb and index finger stack the material in the channel created by their fingertips. The thread then passes up between the thumb and

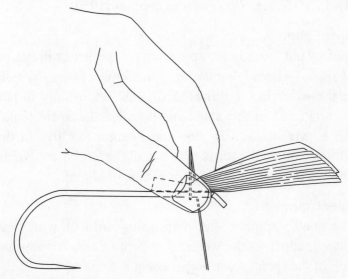

The soft-loop

the material, loops softly over the material, and travels down between the material and the index finger. The thread then firmly snugs down over the material. This is repeated with continuous lateral pressure of thumb and index finger. Further wraps finally secure the material.

Sp.
Abbreviation used when referring to a particular or unknown species in a given genus; the plural form *spp.* is used when referring to several species.

Spade hackle
These rounded back feathers take their name from the shape of a digging spade. The spade hackle comes from the scapulars, which are between the back and the wing. Sometimes the medium coverts are also called spades. The spades furnish nymph legs, nymph cases, and sometimes beards and soft hackles. According to George Leonard Herter's *Professional Fly Tying, Spinning and Tackle Making* (1971), the spade hackle is the shoulder hackle of a bird. "There are broad spade-shaped hackles on the shoulders of cocks which produce beautiful whisks for floaters" (G. E. M. Skues, *Silk, Fur and Feather* [1950]).

Spent gnat
In England, usually the spent mayfly spinner or imitation of such. "After laying her eggs the female *[May fly]* falls in the water in the throes of dissolution, usually in late evening, and in this stage she is called the Spent Gnat" (G. E. M. Skues, *Silk, Fur and Feather* [1950]). In the United States, the term *gnat* usually refers to any small Diptera of the genus *Culex* or genus *Simulium*.

Spent spinner
The mayfly spinner after ovipositing and with wings extended, adrift on the water; the spent imago. Also imitation of the spent, waterborne insect.

Spider

A hackle fly or soft-hackle fly (See *Soft-hackle*); a sparsely hackled, wet fly; a pattern style, traditionally wet, tied with a short body and one or two wraps (seldom more) of a long, shoulder hackle; "Spider-flies or, as they are often called, hackle or buzz flies are held in high repute. . . " (W. C. Stewart, *The Practical Angler* [1919]). In the United States, the term usually refers to an artificial dry fly with extended hackle and tail proportions tied on a light-wire hook. Such a pattern falls gently to water, elevates the hook above the surface, and drifts with less drag over intricate currents. "Fly types which are similar to the spider are the variant, a long, hackled fly of conventional design featuring wings and body, and a skater, a spider without a tail" (A. J. McClane, *McClane's Standard Fishing Encyclopedia* [1965]).

According to Harold Smedley, in *Fly Patterns and Their Origins* (1950), "The present day palmer is hackled full length, while the modern spider is long hackled at the head only." Smedley also notes that "Many refer to tying of hackles directly to the hook as the Michigan style." W. C. Stewart, in *The Practical Angler* (1919), described the "spider" and recommended that the soft, sparsely tied hackle barbs equal total hook length. Stewart divided all flies as either winged or spiders. In *Yorkshire Trout Flies* (1885), T. E. Pritt gives the rationale for the pattern design: "It is far more difficult to imitate a perfect insect and to afterwards impart to it a semblance of life in or on the water, than it is to produce something which is sufficiently near to resemblance of an imperfectly developed insect, struggling to attain the surface of the stream. Trout undoubtedly take a hackled fly for the insect just rising from the pupa in a half-drowned state; and the opening and closing of the fibres of the feathers give it an appearance of vitality." Also the spider fly *(Tipula oleracea)* in James Rennie's *Alphabet of An-*

gling (1849) and the Spider Fly or Gravel Bed *(Anisomera obscura),* a Tipulidae, in Alfred Ronalds's *The Fly-Fisher's Entomology* (1844). See *Soft-hackled fly* in *Proportions.*

Spinner

(1) The sexually mature adult mayfly, the imago; apparently, perhaps so called because of the "spinning" or gyrating nuptial flights of the adult mayfly. "A spinner is a done dun" (Harold Smedley, *Fly Patterns and Their Origins* [1950]). (2) An imitation of the sexually mature adult mayfly. "One or other of several flies, or imitations of these, used especially in trout-fishing (1787)" *(OED).*

The term *spinner* has a complex history. John Betts believes that the term may have first come from the seemingly whirling wings of the cranefly. Some early angling authors did call the large Diptera *spinners.* Apparently, the term first appears in the first edition of Thomas Best's *The Art of Angling* (1787). Certainly his Red Spinner—a tailless palmer with red seal fur mixed with bear hair, gold twist, starling wing, and red cock hackle, which "kills very well till the latter end of August"—is more cranefly than mayfly. Michael Theakson, in *British Angling Flies* (1883), reclassified angling insects according to private caprice. All mayflies, regardless of size, became *drakes.* Caddis became *duns.* Stoneflies became *browns,* and craneflies (Diptera) become *spinners.* This is why Theakson calls Alfred Ronalds's Gravel Bed (Spider Fly), which is a Tipulidae, a Gravel Spinner. John Waller Hills calls Theakson's aberrant classification "a tiresome nomenclature." Theakson's unique language limited his influence. Unfortunately, Louis Rhead followed Theakson's nomenclature in *American Trout Stream Insects* (1914). Like Theakson, Rhead calls all craneflies *spinners* and all nymphs or larvae *creepers.*

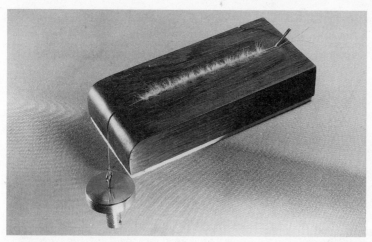

A traditional spinning block with single-hook whirl. The far side notch separates the thread loop for loading. After loading and prior to spinning, the "notch" thread lies directly on top of the "channel" thread, capturing dubbing or fibers.

Spinning block

The spinning block, created by Dick Clark and illustrated in James E. Leisenring's *The Art of Tying the Wet Fly* (1971), consists of a small, hardwood block that accepts a dubbing loop. Brads hold the dubbing loop that is then positioned in a central groove. "The waxed thread is looped over the headless brads and secured in knife-cuts in the close-grained hardwood block leaving both hands free to arrange the dubbing. Then the right hand thread is laid over the dubbing along the shallow groove, and all are twisted to make a fly body." The spinning block, also known as a dubbing block, was Clark's answer to Leisenring's dubbing method that required sophisticated fingering to create a dubbing rope by rolling it on the trouser leg.

Spinning hook
See *Hackle pliers.*

Spinning knot

This knot connects the fly to the tippet. It can be tied in 10
seconds and—once the tippet passes through the hook
eye—in total darkness. Unlike some knots, the smaller the
fly pattern, the easier it is to tie. This knot, similar to a reversed Duncan loop, is spun in the "loom" of the hand. For
greater strength, the tippet may be looped twice through
the eye or once around the shank. With brief practice, the
result is a swift and sure knot. The spinning knot, like all
knots, should be tied in a smooth, continuous movement.

1. After passing the tippet through the eye of the fly,
   hold the tippet end or tag between the thumb and
   forefinger of the left hand. With the right thumb and
   forefinger, slide the fly down the tippet.

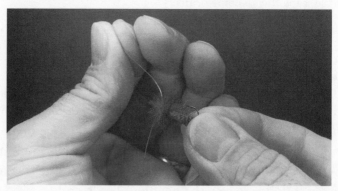

2. Pass the fly across the left palm, over the little finger,
   and behind the back of the left hand. Then, draw the

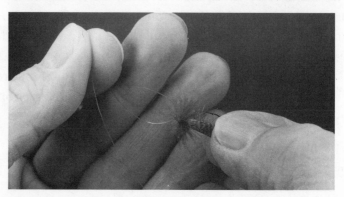

fly *(with the fly riding on the tippet loop)* between the index and middle finger of the left hand.

3. Spin, in either direction, the looped fly five or more times around the tippet section held taut in the left palm. Arc the fingers to create spinning space and to keep the tippet taut.

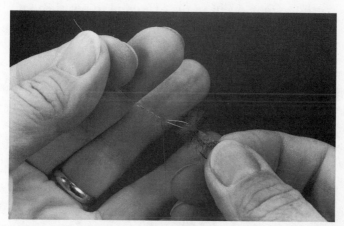

4. With the fly in the right hand and while still holding the tag end of the tippet between the left thumb and the index finger, relax and remove the "loop fingers" from the loop. Continue to hold the tippet tag as the fingers rotate to grasp the wraps made around the tippet.

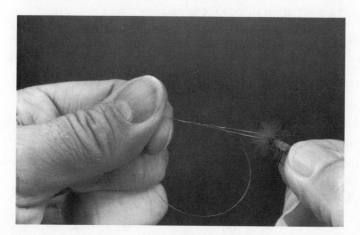

5. Now, with the right hand, slowly pull the fly *away from* the knot. To minimize tippet waste, do not pull the tippet tag. Once the knot has been loosely drawn, continue to pull the fly, sliding the knot against the hook eye. Snug the knot firmly against the eye. If the knot is tightened before it snugs against the eye, then a crinkle may occur in the extended tippet. The knot must be *loosely formed* before it is drawn against the hook eye. Finally, trim excess.

Spiracles
Breathing pores of insects; the external opening on the body wall of an insect for breathing.

Sprig or sprigging
"Small projecting part or point, 1679" *(OED)*. "Minutely branched, 1714" *(OED)*. ". . . And a sprig or two of pheasant tail" (William Blacker's *The Art of Fly-Making, Angling and Dyeing of Colours* [1855]). "Let the toppings extend two-eighths of an inch longer than the other sprigging" (Quoted by W. H. Lawrie in *A Reference Book of English Trout Flies* [1967]).

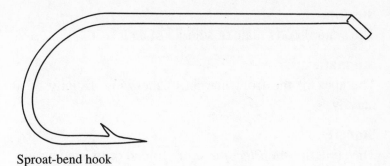

Sproat-bend hook

Sproat

A hook bend characterized by a semiangular shape, one of the most common hook shapes in fly tying. "An admirable hook is one called the Sproat bend, being the invention of Mr. Sproat, of Ambleside" (Francis Francis, *A Book on Angling* [1876]). The disadvantage, though a minor one, of the Sproat bend is the significant amount of hook heel that extends beyond the fly body; however, for wet flies, bucktails, and streamers, the extension poses no problems. The Sproat bend has more bite than a perfect bend, and the gradual curve between the heel and shank makes the Sproat a relatively strong hook design. See *Hook (nomenclature)*.

Stadia

The nymphal period between molts; said of insects.

Staring

"Of hair, a horse's coat, feathers, fibres of any kind: to stand on end. Now chiefly technical. 1523" *(OED)*. "The Body black, and wrapped with a red feather of a Capon untrim'd, that is, the whole length of the Hackle staring out" (James Chetham, *The Angler's Vade Mecum* [1700]).

Sternite

The ventral body plate or sclerite of an insect.

Stigmatic area

The apex of the front margin of the wing, usually of a mayfly.

Stonefly

The stonefly (the *Plecoptera* or "folded or twisted wing" fly, from Greek *plektos* = twisted) has a head and thorax with a combined length that nearly equals that of the abdomen. The abdomen has ten segments, with nine clearly discernable. Each thoracic section has a pair of legs terminating in the two-clawed tarsus. A pair of wings is rooted in each of the two rear thoracic sections. The ventral thoracic area carries the filamentous gills. The placement of the hair gills is one index to speciation. The nymphs have two whiplike tails, segmented and slightly shorter than the abdomen. However, in some genera, the tails are noticeably longer than the abdomen.

The nymphs are primarily herbivorous, living on riparian plants; but, depending on species and available food, predaceous activity is found among some senior instars (the nymphs immediately before emergence). The nymphs are easily distinguished by the absence of abdominal gills; only the 2-inch *Pteronarcys* will have minor strand gills on the first few abdominal segments. The nymphs usually have one subaquatic year; however, the larger species, like the *Pteronarcys californica,* may have three. The nymphs crawl and clamber among the rocks. Their swimming ability is minimal; they are best imitated with an upstream tension drift or a teasing dead drift.

An early stonefly pattern appears in the *Treatyse* (1496): "The stone flye, the body of blacke wull & yelowe under the wynge, and under the tayle & wynges of the drake." Charles Cotton, in *The Complete Angler,* follows this with a stonefly made of brown and yellow camlet mixed with bear's dun "so placed that your Flie may be more yellow on the belly and towards the tail beneath, than in any other part, and you are to place two or three hairs of a black cat's beard on the top of the hook in your arming, so as to be turned up, when you wrap on your dubbing, and to stand almost upright, and staring one from another, and note that your Flie is to be ribbed with yellow silk, and the wings long, and very large, of the dark grey feather of the mallard." The stonefly, according to Cotton is "bred of a Cadis" and when it "has not the patience to continue in his crust or hulk," emerges on some stone, "at which time we call him a Jack." The stonefly had various names, including creeper and water cricket. W. C. Stewart, in *The Practical Angler* (1919), notes that two flies are called the May-fly: the green drake and the stonefly. *May-fly*, evidently, was a term for the stonefly on the Tweed and in the border districts. This explains why Stewart concludes that the creeper or water cricket is the "May-fly in its embryo state." Stewart's lengthy description of the stonefly, commonly called a creeper, is remarkably detailed and knowledgeable.

The notable hatch of the "salmon fly" *(P. californica)* on the Madison River in Montana begins about the end of the first week in June at Three Forks and moves upstream. The hatch arrives about the fourth of July at Ennis, appears about the fourteenth of July at McAtee Bridge, and finishes during the last week of the month at Slide Inn. The 3-year-old *P. californica* develops rapidly in the warm waters of spring and migrates to the slack shallows, where it crawls out on rocks and other objects. The cranial suture splits, and the adult emerges. The nymphs will emerge for a couple of days on any particular stream location as the hatch slowly moves upstream. Such mass hatching provokes active rises from Madison trout. The Sofa Pillow, originated by Pat Barnes of West Yellowstone, is one of the many successful patterns for the large stonefly nymph. Besides his floating nymph for the egg-laying adult stonefly, Dave Whitlock, in *The Second Fly-Tyer's Almanac* (with Robert Bolye, 1978), has produced a soft stonefly nymph that imitates the nymphs immediately after their periodic ecdysis or molting.

The Perlidae (gills on the three thoracic sections), Nemouridae (diverging wing pods), Capniidae (wide metathoracic pods), and Pteronarcidae (abdominal segments one to two or thirteen-branch gilled, *An Introduction to the Aquatic Insects of North America,* K. W. Cummins and R. W. Merritt [1978]) are common in the Western United States. The Perlidae, one of the largest stonefly families, are predominately carnivorous. The Pteronarcidae begin to emerge in April, but not in the numbers associated with the Madison. The Western Sally (*Isoperla spp.* and similar) is common in the Northwest United States and comparable to its English namesake on the riffle waters of Shropshire. In *Rough Stream Trout Flies* (1976), by Taff Price, there is a Welsh border pattern for the Yellow Sally: pale yellow wool body and pale ginger hackle on a size 14. Other dusty yellow nymph patterns can prove effective for these smaller stoneflies.

Stonefly Nymph Characteristics

1. A distinct head, thorax, and abdomen
2. Six legs, each terminated by two claws
3. Two distinct and separated whiplike tails
4. Distinct, segmented antennae
5. Gills absent, or filamentous gills beneath the thorax and between the legs
6. Ten distinct abdominal segments, usually oval or circular in cross section

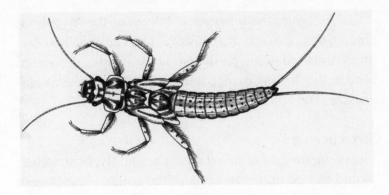

7. Inferior swimmers that either arch the body or assume the fetal position when adrift
8. Instars vary from twenty-two to thirty-three, with a nymphal period from 1 to 3 years
9. Two pairs of wing pads

Stonefly Adult Characteristics

1. The general appearance of a squat "aquatic cockroach" with wings tight and flat above the abdomen
2. Four equal-length, prominently veined wings
3. When airborn, a near-vertical body attitude and a heavy, fluttering flight
4. Three tarsal segments

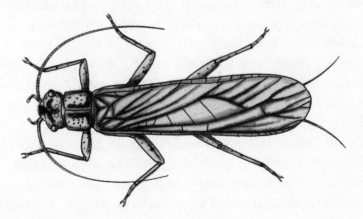

In fly tying, the imitative elements of the nymph include size, color, and drift attitude. Drift attitude is sometimes imitated with particular hook bends: the round bend or the drifting nymph hook. Most adult patterns emphasize size, color, and large downwings.

Stretcher

The point, trail, or terminal fly. "The end fly, or stretcher, should be tied on the last link of the collar. . . . It is very doubtful too, what the trout imagines this red fly [a red fly with gold twist] to be, probably some worm or grub, and if so, it would be more naturally used as an end fly, when it is often or generally under water, than bobbing and dapping about the surface of the water, as the middle or bob fly must do" (H. C. Cutcliffe, *The Art of Trout Fishing on Rapid Streams* [1863]). "The usual way in fly-fishing is to have one fly on the end of the line, termed *stretcher,* and one or more, termed *droppers,* hanging from the line behind the stretcher by a length of link sufficient to let them just tip the water when the line is a little raised and drawn along" (James Rennie, *Alphabet of Angling* [1849]). "When you use more than one fly, the farthest is called the stretcher; the others are called drop-flies" (J. March, *The Jolly Angler* [1842]). "The droppers are attached to bits of stouter gut than the cast (to keep from fouling it) about 4 inches long called dropper points which are tied on at right angles to [the cast or leader]" (W. S. Jackson, *Notes of a Fly Fisher: An Attempt at a Grammar of the Art* [1933]). According to Jackson, the lower dropper is about 3 feet above the tail fly. The second dropper should be about 2 feet or 2 feet, 6 inches above the lower dropper. The dropper points should not be longer than 3 or 4 inches with the fly attached. If three flies are used, the three stages of insect may be imitated: the heavier tail fly may be a nymph or

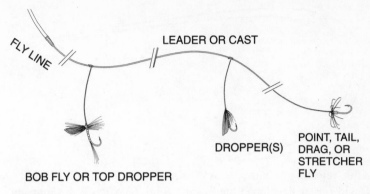

Stretcher

pupa, the lower dropper may be an emerger, and the top dropper a dry fly. With two flies attached, the tail fly may be nymph, pupa, or wet, and the higher dropper a dry fly. The dry fly then acts as a strike indicator for the sunken fly. "The heaviest wire [hook] ought invariably to form the trail-fly; that which is lighter being disposed of, at due distance, as a bob or dropper" (Thomas Tod Stoddart, *The Angler's Companion* [1853]). See *Whip*.

Strip wing
A salmon-fly wing that consists of strips made from one type of feather only. See *Mixed wing*.

Suture
The flexible seam that connects the body plates of an insect.

Swan bend (hook making)
A grayling hook characterized by an advanced bend and spear that is completely covered or concealed by the shank or the fly body. The most abrupt part of the bend lies near the hook shank. "There has long been a want felt of a suitable hook for grayling, to be at once light, durable, and effective in shape and make. Many experi-

After rejecting "clumsy, heavy" trout hooks for grayling fishing, David Foster developed the "swan" bend. S. Allcock & Company Limited of Redditch produced Foster's hook in grayling and salmon sizes. A similar bend also appears as "an old-fashioned lip-hook" in H. Cholmondeley-Pennell's *Fishing,* 1886.

ments we have tried in years past with the view of surmounting this difficulty, but failure was the characteristic feature of each, until we accidentally hit upon a particular bend, which was found to work with unusual success. . . . This hook has been designated the 'swan' bend, and as such it is known amongst the few anglers who have hitherto kept it secret" (David Foster, *The Scientific Angler* [undated]).

Swedish hook

A hook bend characterized by an angular shank loop (for mounting a parachute hackle) with the eye wire returning

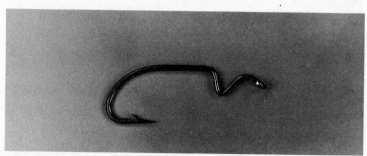

Swedish hook

to the shank line. The dressed hook is designed to float with the point on top and without water penetration, producing a more realistic float angle. Nils E. Eriksson and Gunnar Johnson of Sweden created the design while Partridge & Sons produced the hook in 1979.

Swim

The area or range that an angler manages when fishing. ". . . Properly speaking, it only comprehends the distance within reach of your rod and line, from where you have taken your stand for angling, which no honest angler out [sic] to intrude on" (J. March, *The Jolly Angler* [c. 1842]).

Tarsal claw
The claw at the apex of the tarsus on insects.

Tarsus
The final leg segment of an insect, the tarsal claw joins distally; the tarsus contains one to five segments, often a consideration in taxonomy (*tarsi,* plural).

Taxonomy
The science of classification; Usually a binomial system of classification, often descriptive and referring to size, color, habits, or morphology, which includes a capitalized genus name and a lowercase species or subspecies name, for instance, *Epeorus longimanus.* Note that genus names and higher are capitalized. The suffix *-idae* indicates a family, as in Baetidae; the suffix *-inae* indicates a subfamily, as in Hydrophilinae; other endings are *-oidea* for superfamily and *-ini* for tribe. Species and subspecies derived from geological names are formed by adding the genitive or adjectival endings such as *-ae, -icus, -ica,*

-icum, -ensis, or *-ense;* the taxonomic order is phylum, class, order, family, genus, and species, with various subdivisions. The terms are usually derived from Latin and Greek, but may also come from other languages, as well as from people and place names. Genus and species names are always italicized or underlined.

The terms *fly* and *bug* have specialized meanings. When fly is written *separately,* such as black fly, the insect belongs to the order Diptera. When the word fly is written *together* with the descriptive word, such as mayfly and stonefly, then the insect is in an order other than the Diptera. In like manner, the *true* bugs of the order Hemiptera use bug as a *separate* term, such as water bug. Insects in other orders use bug *together* with the descriptive term, such as sowbug.

The basic rules for scientific pronunciation include:

1. All vowels in scientific names are pronounced.
2. A vowel at the end of a word has a long sound, except when it is an **a,** then it has an **uh** sound (the schwa "murmur vowel" of unstressed syllables; the sound of **a** in the word **above**).
3. The vowel in the final syllable of a word has a short sound, except **es,** which is pronounced **ease (eez).**
4. In words beginning with **ps, pt, ct, cn, gn,** or **mn,** the initial letter is silent, but when these letters appear together in the middle of a word, the first letter is pronounced.

The following list contains common insect names and their various pronunciations. Some terms are commonly pronounced several different ways.

Acroneuria: ak-row-**NEAR**-ee-uh
Accentrella: a-sen-**TRELL**-uh
Adoptiva: adop-**TEE**-vuh

Albertae: al-**BER**-tay
Allectus: ah-**LECK**-tus
Alternatus: alter-**NATE**-us
Ameletus: am-ah-**LAY**-tus, am-ah-**LEE**-tus
atracaudata: atra-caw-**DATE**-uh
atratus: ah-**TRAIT**-us
attenella: at-**TEN**-ella
attenuata: ah-**TEN**-you-**AH**-tuh
Baetidae: **BEE**-ti-dee, **BAY**-ti-dee, **BAIT**-ah-day,
    BAIT-ah-dee
Baetis: **BEE**-tiss, **BAY**-tiss, **BAIT**-iss
Baetisca: bay-**TISK**-ah, bee-**TISS**-kah
Baetiscidae: bay-**TISK**-ah-day, bay-**TISK**-ah-dee
Bicaudatus: by-caw-**DATE**-us
Bicolor: **BY**-color
Bicornuta: by-kor-**NEW**-tuh
Brachycentridae: brak-ee-**CEN**-tri-dee
Brachycentrus: brak-ee-**CEN**-truss
Brachycercus: bra-key-**SIR**-cus
Brachyptera: brah-**KIP**-tur-uh
Caenidae: **SEE**-ni-dee, **CANE**-ah-day, **CANE**-ah-dee
Caenis: **SEE**-niss, **CAY**-niss, **CANE**-iss
Callibaetis: cal-li-**BEE**-tiss, caley-**BAY**-tiss
Canadense: can-uh-**DEN**-see, can-ah-**DEN**-say
Capnia: **CAP**-nee-uh
Centroptilum: sen-trop-**TILL**-um
Cheumatopsyche: chew-mat-uh-**SIGH**-kee
Chimarra: shi-**MAR**-ruh
Chironomid: ki-**RON**-o-mid, ki-ro-**NO**-mid
Chironomidae: ki-ro-**NO**-mi-dee
Chloroperla: klor-oh-**PURR**-luh
Cingulatus: sing-you-**LATE**-us, sin-goo-**LAH**-tus
Cinygmula: sin-ig-**MULE**-ah
Cloeon: clow-**EE**-on
Cornuta: cor-**NEW**-tuh

Cornutella: core-new-**TELL**-ah

Deceptivus: de-**SEPT**-ee-vus, de-sep-**TEE**-vus

Deficiens: dee-**FISS**-ee-ens, deh-**FISS**-ee-uns

Diaphanus: die-ah-**FANE**-us

Dicosmoecus: die-koss-**MEE**-cuss

Doddsi: **DODDS**-eye

Epeorus: ee-pee-**OR**-us

Ephemera: *f*-uh-**MUR**-uh, ee-**FE**-mur-a, uh-**FEM**-ura

Ephemerella: *f*-uh-mur-**REL**-uh, eh-fem-uh-**REL**-luh

Ephemerellidae: *f*-uh-mur-**REL**-li-dee,
     eh-fem-uh-**REL**-li-dee

Ephemeridae: *f*-uh-**MARE**-i-dee, eh-fem-uh-**REE**-dee

Ephemeroptera: *f*-uh-mur-**OP**-tur-uh,
     ee-fem-ur-**OP**-tur-uh

Flavilinea: flah-vil-**LYNN**-ee-uh

Fuscum: **FUSS**-come

Futile: few-**TILL**-ee

Glacialis: glay-see-**ALICE**

Glossosoma: gloss-ah-**SO**-ma

Glossosomatidae: gloss-ah-so-**MAT**-ah-dee

Grandis: **GRAN**-diss

Guttulata: goo-ta-**LAW**-tah

Hageni: **HOG**-en-eye

Hecuba: **HECK**-you-bah, he-**KYOU**-bah

Heptagenia: hep-tuh-**JEAN**-ee-uh

Heptageniidae: hep-tuh-guh-**NEE**-i-dee

Hexagenia: hex-uh-**JEAN**-ee-uh

Hilaris: hill-**AIR**-us

Hydropsyche: high-drop-**SIGH**-kee

Hydropsychidae: high-drop-**SIGH**-ki-dee,
     high-drop-**SIGH**-key-day

Hydroptila: high-**DROP**-till-uh

Hydroptilidae: high-drop-**TI**-li-dee

Inermis: in-**ER**-miss

Infrequens: in-**FREAK**-whens, in-**FREE**-qwens

Invaria: in-**VAIR**-ee-uh, in-**VAR**-ee-uh

Isogenus: eye-sow-**GEE**-nus

Isonychia: eye-so-**NICK**-ee-uh

Isoperla: eye-sow-**PURR**-luh

Lepidostoma: leh-pi-**DOSS**-tuh-muh

Lepidostomatidae: lep-i-doss-toe-**MAH**-ti-dee

Leptophlebia: lept-oh-**FLEE**-bee-uh,
   lep-toh-**FLEE**-bee-uh

Leptophlebiidae: lep-toe-fluh-**BEE**-i-dee,
   lept-oh-flee-**BEE**-ah-day

Leuctra: **LUKE**-truh

Limnephilidae: lim-nuh-**PHIL**-i-dee

Limnephilus: lim-nuh-**PHIL**-us

Lineatus: line-**EE**-a-tus

Longimanus: lon-ge-**MAN**-us, lon-je-**MAN**-us

Minutus: my-**NEW**-tuss

Mollis: **MALL**-us

Nemouridae: neh-**MOOR**-i-dee

Neocloeon: knee-oh-**KLOW**-ee-on

Paraleptophlebia: para-lep-toh-**FLEE**-bee-uh

Perlidae: **PURR**-li-dee

Perlodidae: purr-**LOW**-di-dee

Plecoptera: plee-**COP**-tur-uh

Potamanthus: pot-uh-**MAN**-thus, pot-uh-**MANTH**-us

Pteronarcidae: tare-oh-**NAR**-si-dee

Pteronarcys: tare-oh-**NAR**-seez

Rhithrogena: rith-roe-**GEE**-nuh, rye-throw-**JEAN**-uh

Rhyacophila: rye-uh-**CAW**-phil-uh

Rhyacophilidae: rye-uh-koe-**PHIL**-i-dee

Simulans: sim-**YULE**-ans

Siphlonurus: sif-low-**NUR**-us

Stenonema: sten-oh-**KNEE**-muh

Taeneopteryx: tea-nee-**OPP**-tur-ix

Tricaudatus: try-caw-**DATE**-us

Trichoptera: try-**COP**-tur-uh

Tricorythodes: try-cor-ee-**THO**-deez
Varia: **VAIR**-ee-uh, **VAR**-ee-uh
Vicarium: vie-**CARE**-ee-um, vie-**CAR**-ee-um
Wormaldia: worm-**ALL**-dee-uh

Teneral adult
In the Odonata, the recently emerged pale adult before full coloration; from the Latin *tener,* meaning tender.

Tergite
A back body plate of an insect; a dorsal sclerite.

Tewed
"The tawing of leather. To work anything into proper consistency by beating. 1440" *(OED).* "Badgers Skin Hair . . . is very good Dubbing, after the Skin is tewed in the Skinners Lime-pits" (James Chetham, *The Angler's Vade Mecum* [1700]).

Thermocline
See *Epilimnion.*

Thermotropism
The response to temperature.

Thigmotropism
The response to touch; the trout that avoids direct contact with objects in the water is said to be negatively thigmotropic.

Throstle
"A thrush, esp. the song-thrush or mavis, *Turdus musicus.* Now only literary and dialectical" *(OED).* "The wings are made of a woodcock's feather, or the underpart of a throstle, or fieldfare's wing" (Charles Bowlker, *The Art of Angling* [1839]).

Tibia
The fourth segment of an insect leg connected between the femur and tarsus; (*tibiae,* plural).

Tippet

The terminal leader section to which the fly is tied, probably derived from Late Middle English *tippe,* meaning tip, end, tail, or slender extremity. A long, narrow strip of cloth usually worn hanging from the hood or sleeve (thirteenth century) (Joseph T. Shipley, *Dictionary of Early English* [1968]). The level line or tippet section tied to the smaller terminus of a leader. The term *cast* is used in English angling for the word *tippet.* "*Angling:* a. A length of twisted hair or gut forming part of a fishing line. b. Part of an artificial fly. 1825" *(OED).* Also the hackle fibers of a golden pheasant, hence "golden pheasant tippet fibers."

Towght

A link, length, or section of an angler's horsehair line.

Tracheal gills

The plumose gills of the nymph; the respiratory gills or tubes of an insect.

Traditionalism

See *Imitation.*

Trochanter

The second section of an insect leg connected between the coxa and the femur. See *Insect (nomenclature).*

Tube fly

Streamer flies that have bodies and wings dressed on a length of plastic, nylon, or metal tube. The leader passes through the tube and attaches to the appropriate hook. There are several advantages to a tube fly. First, a tube fly may be light (nylon tube and light hook) or heavy (brass or copper tube and heavy hook). Second, broken hooks are readily replaced. Third, various pattern colors and sizes may be created by using two or more tube flies. Finally, different hook sizes may be used for the same

Tube fly

pattern. According to William F. Blades in *Fishing Flies and Fly Tying* (1962), Native North Americans used hollow bones to create tube flies. George Leonard Herter, in *Professional Fly Tying, Spinning and Tackle Making* (1971) describes the bone tube fly: "When such a streamer is drawn through the water, a fan-like bunch of bubbles continually leaves the end of the bone. Although these bone streamers are effective as they are, a few small hackle feathers or a little hair tied onto the outside of the bone increases their effectiveness." Tube patterns are now offered to various fresh and saltwater game fish.

Tubercles
The rounded nodules—a knoblike body elevation—of an insect.

Turbinate
The shape like an inverted, truncated cone, often stalked; said of the stalked, turbanlike eyes of some insects.

Umbrella hackle

Spider patterns of Northern Italy with a hackle tied concave or dull-side forward, i.e., toward the hook eye. The radiating barbs extend over and beyond the hook eye. Such a pattern is usually tied off behind the hackle, thus encouraging advanced barbs forward. The pattern has "kick" as the forward barbs contort with current movement. Similar reverse-hackle patterns are found in France. "[Aimé] Devaux used two hackles in order to thicken the collar and improve the float. The fibers of the rear hackle are bent forward by the finishing knot made at the shoulder of the shank. This type of dressing, which is found on most of the dry flies of Devaux, is called 're-verse' or 'umbrella' dressing. It is designed to prevent the hackle from lying back after use" (Jean-Paul Pequegnot, *French Fishing Flies* [1987]).

Underfur

The fine, dense hair near the hair base of fur bearers; the soft, basal hair; the vellus. See *Fur*.

Unguentum piscatorum mirabile (angling)

An ointment that "prodigiously causes Fish to bite," according to James Chetham's *The Angler's Vade Mecum* (1700): "Of Man's Fat, Cats Fat, Herons Fat, and of the best *Affa-foetida* ["a Gummy Juice of Laser, Laserpitium, or Sylphyon"], of each two Drams, Cummin seed finely powdered two Scruples, and of Camphor, Galbanum and Venice Turpentine, of each one Dram, Civet grains two, make according to Art, all into an indifferent thin Oyntment, with the Chymical Oyls of Lavender, Annise and Cammomil, of each an equal quantity." Chetham, a late contemporary of Walton, augmented his splendid patterns with various abhorrent ointments. Man's fat was procured from London *chyrurgeons* (surgeons) specializing in anatomy, and heron's fat from poulterers. Chetham "forbore (for some Reasons) to insert" the ointment in his first edition. Apparently, it was extremely difficult to keep a good jewel hidden. "But now, since it is divulged, [I] value it not the less, but esteem it as a jewel." To attract fish, the ointment was applied to the last 8 inches of line near the hook. Other curious ointments included the marrow from a heron's thigh bone, grave earth, powder from the bones or skull of a dead man at the opening of a grave, and mummy powder. Various ointments appear in other early angling books. As John Waller Hills noted in *A History of Fly Fishing for Trout* (1971), "The older fishermen had some advantage over us."

Univoltine

Having but one brood or hatch a year; said of insects.

Variant

Any feather or cape with more than one color; also a fly pattern with extended proportions, especially tail and hackle. "Some fishermen maintain that the name *[variant]* was derived from the fact that the hackle is composed of two lengths of fibres. The more popular accepted view is that the first 'variant' was tied by Doctor Baigent of Great Britain 'the fly being first introduced as Baigent's Variant of the Poole Hackle.' Since its development in a pattern calling for a gold body and long, rusty dun hackle, the term 'variant' has been taken to mean any fly that is tied in the general manner" (William B. Sturgis, *Fly-Tying* [1940]). The Baigent patterns were thought to mimic the optical effects of floating insects. Because of their soft landing and delicate, drifting presentation, Preston Jennings believed that they were particularly appropriate for brown trout (*A Book of Trout Flies* [1935]). The original Variants were usually dressed with tinsel bodies and oversize hackles. With protracted hackle barbs, Variants could be skated across the surface to attract trout.

Veer a line

"Let it [the line] off the reel after striking" (Thomas Best, *The Art of Angling* [1822]).

Veinlets

The short, detached, and narrow veins occurring along the trailing margin of some insect wings. Veinlets are common characteristics of the *Baetis* mayfly wing. See also *Marginal intercalary veins* and *Cubital intercalary veins.*

Vellus

The short, fine, "down" hair of a mammal. The soft underfur. See *Underfur.*

Ventral

The belly or bottom side; the underside.

Vise

A jawed tool that holds a hook when fly tying. Vises differ according to jaw mechanism (draw cam, push cam, spring lever, and screw knob), mounting systems (C-clamp, table base, screw mount, handheld), and materials (usually brass, steel, aluminum). D. H. Thompson is credited with the invention of the collet vise, with a single cam lever that closes or opens the jaws. It is generally recommended that tyers mount a hook in a vise with the shank level or horizontal and with the point and barb exposed. However, William B. Sturgis and Eric Taverner, in *New Lines for Fly-Fishers* (1946), recommend that tyers "insert the hook in the vise, with the shank inclined upwards and to the right, at an angle of 10°." The slight cant prevents the thread from slipping off the hook while tying.

Fly-Tying Vise Features

1. Vise should accept the standard range of hooks with minimal adjustments for maximum hold. Vise jaws with grooves, serrations, or pins for holding and positioning hooks should position hooks securely.
2. Vise shape should allow adequate access to the hook when tying. Jaw shape should allow adequate access to shank and exposed bend.
3. Threads should be fine, deep, and acutely angled to prevent back-off of adjustments. Lock rings may be added to snug adjustment rings. All knurling should be clean and precise.
4. Vise should have a stable and secure mounting system.
5. If required, the vise should accept supplementary tools, such as gallows, material clip, and bobbin cradle. A standard diameter stand-rod, usually 3/8 inch, should accept future products, even from different manufacturers.
6. All functions—jaw closure, jaw adjustment, jaw rotation, jaw angle—should be effortless and convenient to perform. No extra tools should be required to mount or adjust the vise head.

The straight pin vise with brass C-clamp was typical of many nineteenth-century tying vises. Such vises, in fact, were used well into the twentieth century. G. E. M. Skues, the English angler who had a way with nymphs, used a small vise held in his mouth by a horn plate. All tying took place about 6 inches from his face. As awkward as this sounds, it was an ingenious solution to field tying. In 1909, Hardy marketed a vise that either clipped to the thumb or screwed into the table. Later John Veniard Limited sold the Croyden hand vise, a diminutive looped-handle pin vise with a screw-sleeve closure.

At the turn of the century, Frederic M. Halford
lamented that a serviceable vise was not easily procured,
that most were of faulty design and materials and had
wing screws that projected beyond the head to trap the

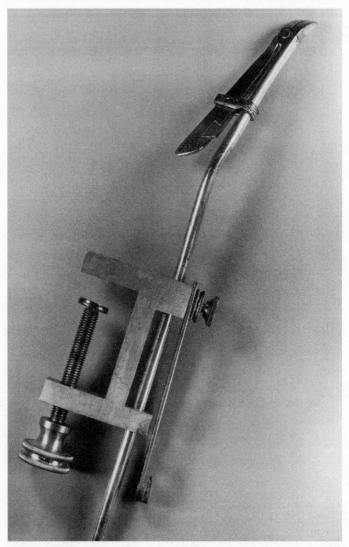

1898 Hawksley's fly-tying vise with attached "Athenian" rubber
silk-clip created by Harry G. McClelland. Like locking pliers, the
collar around the stem and handle slides down, thus clamping the
hook in place.

tying silk. He did advocate, however, their use. "No one, amateur or professional, after once experiencing the advantages of having the hook rigidly held by a process which leaves both hands free, would ever revert to the old and uncomfortable plan of holding the bend of the

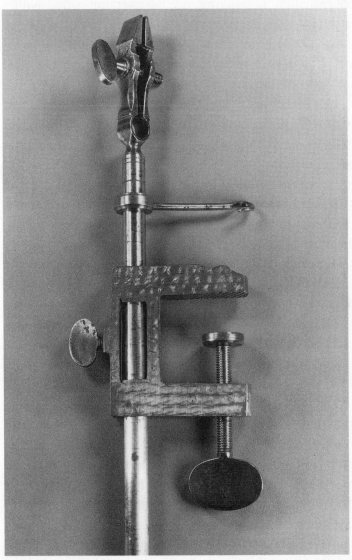

Nineteenth-century, straight pin vise with brass C-clamp and adjustable silk-hook.

hook between the thumb and the forefinger of the left hand throughout the operation of tying." In *Fly-Tying for Salmon* (1942), Eric Taverner insisted that "the silk breaks far more often if the hook is held rigidly in the jaws of a vise." He did concede, however, that some procedures, such as winging, are best accomplished with a stationary vise. He believed that the tension of the tying silk would be more easily judged if the hook were handheld. The debate over vise and viseless tying continued into midcentury.

In 1930, Hardy sold the Hardy-Colin vise, a screw collar vise with an adjustable table clamp. The angled head, "being perfectly plain," prevented the thread from "becoming entangled with parts of the vise whilst working" (*The Best of Hardy's Anglers' Guides* [1982]). The work is held at an angle, which permits both hands to operate with ease. Perhaps the most remarkable tying advancement in the first quarter of the twentieth century was the angled head that allowed finger space behind and beneath the pattern. On some early vises, the wing screw, oddly enough, faced the tyer. In time, most pin vises would have the wing screw on the offside of the vise head and away from the tying path. As late as the 1950s, John Veniard Limited marketed stem vises for salmon and streamer tying.

The 1934 Hardy catalog sold the Amateur Vise, a straight pin vise operated by a wing screw and mounted on an adjustable table clamp. A hook arm screwed into the clamp and a slotted rubber washer held the tying silk. Frederic M. Halford, in *Floating Flies and How to Dress Them* (1886), described the function of the hook arm: "The loose hook immediately above the clamp is intended to be used when twisting and waxing the doubled silk for large flies." The hook was also used for twisting and forming the gut loop whipped on blind-eyed salmon hooks.

Warp

"*Angling:* To fasten (the materials of an artificial fly) to the hook, 1676" *(OED)*. "The body of deep green mohair, warped with light green silk" (Charles Bowlker, *The Art of Angling* [1839]).

Water-fly

According to John Waller Hills, the "Water-flie," resembling "a house-fly on a hook," is the first picture of an artificial fly. The water-fly appears in William Lawson's commentary to John Dennys's *The Secrets of Angling* (second edition, ca. 1652). Lawson's marginalia, which added fly-

The Water-fly (John Dennys's *The Secrets of Angling* [second edition, ca. 1652]).

fishing notes and the first mention of fly casting, erroneously asserted that the water-fly, a "May flie," was "bred of the cod-bait [caddis]." Lawson's description fails, in part, to match the woodcut: "The head is of black silk or haire, the wings of a feather of a mallart, teele, or pickled hen-wing. The body of Crewell according to the moneth for colour, and run about with a black haire: all fastened at the taile, with the thread that fastened the hooke. . . ."

Water knot

Fly fishing's oldest knot dating from *The Treatyse of Fysshynge Wyth an Angle* (1496): "Whan ye haue as many of the lynkys as ye suppose wol suffyse for the length of the lyne: thenne must ye knytte theym to gyder wyth a water knotte or elles a duchys knotte. And whan your knotte is knytte: kytte of þe voyde shorte endes a strawe brede for the knotte. Thus shal ye make youre lynes fayr & fyne." The knot, also known as the surgeon's knot, is described and illustrated in the John Hawkins edition of *The Complete Angler* (1766): "To tye a Water-knot, lay the end of one of your hairs about five

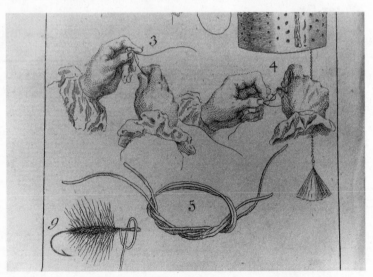

Drawing 5: the water knot (*The Complete Angler* [1766])

inches or less, over that of the other, and through this loop which you would make to tye them in the common way, pass the long and short end of the hairs, which will lie to the right of the loop, twice, and wetting the Knot with your tongue, draw it close, and cut off the spare hair." Notice that there are two turns through the loop and that the knot is wetted before closure. Although not as symmetrical as a blood knot, the water knot is safe and strong when joining different diameters.

Webbing

The dense barbules devoid of barbicels occurring at the feather base and tapering toward the tip: On a dry-fly

The arrow indicates the gray webbing extending along the hackle stem.

hackle, webbing absorbs water and decreases the flotation of the pattern; the interlaced and matted barbules at the center base of the feather. The barbules extend from the barb to form a mat membrane; if barbs (or "fibers") have few or no barbules, the hackle is considered web free. See *Feather (nomenclature)*.

Wet fly

Categorically, any pattern fished beneath the water surface; originally, the wet fly was developed to imitate (1) drowned surface insects, such as duns and spinners; (2) emerging nymphs and pupae; (3) ovipositing adult insects; and (4) small crustaceans and shrimp. Nymphs and streamers, while dressed for subsurface angling, are best considered separately. Traditionally, the wet fly should be dressed sparsely with absorbent materials on a heavy-wire, down-eyed hook. Soft-hackled patterns and variants (spiders) may be considered wet flies. The wet fly, the most antique fly design, usually has matched, tilted quill or barb wings that are tied on last. Though there are notable exceptions, the following elements have been used individually or in combination to characterize a sunk pattern:

1. Any pattern characterized by a heavy or bushy tie of absorbent materials that may include added weight
2. Any pattern in which the wings and hackle fold back or point rearward; any pattern in which the dull or concave side of a soft, hen hackle points to the rear
3. Any pattern with no tail or a short, soft tail
4. Any pattern tied on a heavy, often down-eyed hook
5. Any "flat" pattern or pattern with materials that occupy a single plane congruent with the shank, bend, and point
6. Any pattern tied on a heavy Sproat or Limerick hook, often lacking a forged bend

7. Any pattern with special parts, such as a beard (wet fly and salmon fly) or thorax (nymph and larva)

An artificial fly floats or sinks based on the following characteristics: (1) hook weight, (2) quality and quantity of hackle, (3) hackle stance, (4) dressing (flotant or sink), (5) pattern design, (6) material absorption, (7) drying false casts, (8) total surface area, and (9) tail design and surface area.

Wheel
The herl wrap (such as ostrich or peacock) at the head of a fly. ". . . Form the wheel at the head with two or three turns of black ostrich herl" (James Ogden, *Ogden on Fly Tying* [1887]).

Whip
"The leader, with its flies attached, is generally termed the Whip, the neatness and proper arrangement of which is of much importance. The fly at the end is called the Stretcher, Drag-Fly or Tail-Fly. Those above are the drop flies. Sometimes they are termed 'Bobbers' or 'Droppers' " (Thaddeus Norris, *The American Angler's Book* [1865]).

Whip finisher
A fly-tying tool that wraps one thread several times over another so that the underthread may eventually be tightened to produce the whip-finish head knot. Some whip finishers work by a spring-lever side hook, such as the Thompson or Veniard, or by a rigid side hook, such as the Matarelli. Once mastered, the whip finisher creates head knots with rapidity, control, and pressure during the whip process. According to Marvin Nolte, an early reference to the knot (though not the term *whip finish*) appears in *The Fly Fisher's Guide* (1816) by George C. Bainbridge: ". . . When the fastening off must be effected, by making three or four loose turns of the silk at such a distance

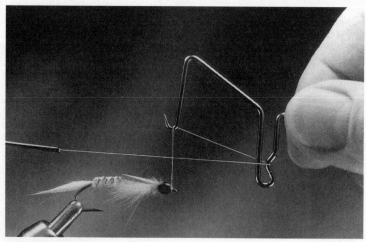

Notice that before wrapping, the thread forms a reversed number "4"; the perpendicular thread will wrap over the horizontal thread with each revolution. Although it makes little difference the direction of the underwraps, a right-handed tyer should *finish* the head by wrapping from the *left* to the *right*. This produces a smooth knot with parallel wraps. Finishing from right to left creates an exposed, diagonal thread crossing over the wraps.

from the hook, as to admit of the end being passed under them, as shewn *[sic]* in *Plate II, fig, 9.*" Frederic M. Halford illustrates the "whip finish" in *Floating Flies and How to Dress Them* (1886). Halford advocates the whip finish over the older method of finishing a fly off with a series of half hitches. According to Thaddeus Norris, in *The American Angler's Book* (1865), this knot is called by some anglers "the invisible knot." This phrase originally came from George C. Bainbridge's *The Fly Fisher's Guide* (1816). Bainbridge illustrates the knot and adds, "The loose turns must then be wrapped closely on the hook, and then the end drawn tight, which will so completely secure the fastening, that if neatly managed, it will be difficult to discover where the fly has been finished. This mode of fastening is called the *invisible knot.*" Norris, who presents a lucid explanation of tying the knot, also uses the knot for attaching gut to hook. T. E. Pryce-Tannatt may have popularized the phrase "whip finish" in *How to Dress Salmon Flies* (1914).

Whirl

The herl; the long barbs with fine, dense fuzz found on the peacock and ostrich tail feathers. "The whirl of an Estridg [ostrich] feather" and "the body made of a whirl of a Peacocks feather" (Izaak Walton, *The Complete Angler* [1766]).

Whisk or wisp

"A slender hair-like or bristle-like part or appendage, as those on the tails of certain insects, 1618" *(OED)*. *Wisps:* "A thin, narrow piece, 1836" *(OED)*. The tail of an artificial fly. Early tyers used a variety of tailing materials, including feather barbs, rabbit whiskers, horsehair, goose biots, and other fibers.

Window, trout window

The diagram and concept of the trout window—based on the optical laws of the angle of incidence and the angle of refraction of trout vision—was first popularized in Alfred Ronalds's *The Fly Fisher's Entomology,* published in 1844. A few later books have continued this research, notably J. W. Dunne's *Sunshine and the Dry Fly* (1924), Col. E. W. Harding's *The Flyfisher & the Trout's Point of View* (1931), Mark Sosin and John Clark's *Through the Fish's Eye* (1973), Vincent Marinaro's *In the Ring of the Rise* (1976), and Brian Clarke and John Goddard's *The Trout and the Fly* (1980).

Early writers usually understood the window in this manner: the 160-degree sight cone of the trout becomes compressed by refraction into a 97-degree cone through which the trout views the world. Yet, the trout does have difficulty seeing beyond the surface mirror. It can see the

The impression of a Callibaetis dun on the mirror. Although the mirror reflects the world beneath the surface, the star-burst of light from the legs and the imprint of the body does appear. Brian Clarke and John Goddard believe that "these star-bursts of light created by the indentation of the feet of the dun floating on the surface . . . are the first triggers to the trout's predatory mechanism" (*The Trout and the Fly* [1980]). The second trip mechanism is the *wings* of the dun as the insect drifts toward the window.

dimpling of hackle feet in the surface, but color and detail are "through a glass darkly." And the *window,* that ring of bright water, is backlit so that again little color and detail is evident. Colonel Harding noted that surface-feeding trout watch beyond the window and recognize the insect by the tiny, surface dimples created by their feet. Like a hunter, the trout follows the "spoor" before it sees the prey. Vincent Marinaro was one of the first modern writers to draw attention to the fact that the trout places the fly at the edge of the window for the purpose of observation. Brian Clarke and John Goddard make reference to *Snell's circle,* the circular boundary between the mirror and window. They argue most convincingly that it is at the ledge of the window that the trout first views the full fly. They also conclude that, when dressing some stillwater nymphs, a reflective strip should be

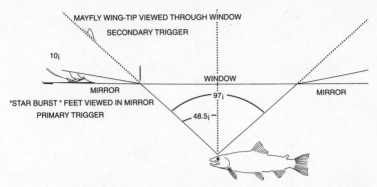

As the mayfly sails into the trout's view, the mirror first reveals the "star-burst" of feet. Shortly thereafter, the wings enter the window.

mounted on the back of the pattern to reflect a spot of light against the otherwise dark background of the mirror.

Wing burners

A metal template that holds feathers or fabric so that a flame, usually a butane-lighter flame, burns the surplus, thereby forming a shaped wing for fly tying. Wing burners come in a variety of wing shapes for adult or nymph, mayfly, caddis, and stonefly wings. Wing burners offer several advantages over wing cutters: (1) a wide variety of sizes and shapes, (2) realistic shapes, and (3) no blades to dull. Because of the blade bend in wing cutters, the widest part is often near the top, unlike many naturals. Cutters work better on synthetics; burners will fuse the wing edges together. For wing burning, select hen feathers that have the barbs at right angles or nearly so. Acutely angled barbs may be burned through at the base, resulting in an angular wing. Wing burner features include:

1. An appropriate wing size and shape
2. A well-matched template edge for a clean, sharp wing shape

The lowered stem of a dun wing minimizes spin or flutter during the casting stroke. Carefully calculate stem placement. Symmetrical stem placement may cause erratic flight. Compare the off-center placement of a flight-feather stem or a sailboat mast. Both are positioned to effectively penetrate the wind. Position the stems as illustrated.

3. The proper metal thickness to prevent warp or fuzzed wing edges
4. An adequate length for cool handling
5. A secure clamping of the wing
6. A variable feather positioning to accommodate dun, thoracic dun, and spinner wings

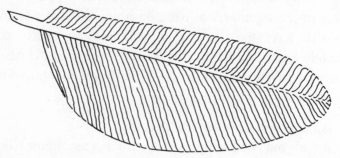

An advanced stem reduces casting flutter.

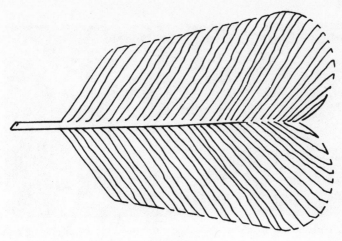

A centered stem for flat nymph wings.

7. A template design that permits various stem angles. If barbs are acutely angled, they may be burned through at the base, resulting in a truncated or abrupt edge.

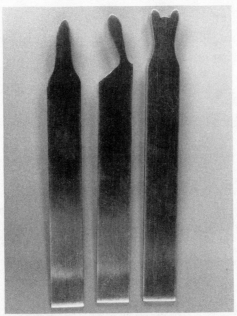

Wing burners (left to right) for adult mayfly wings, adult caddis wings, and stonefly nymph wing pads.

The Yorkshire wing cutter. Note the cut wing and rubber cutting pad.

Wing cutter
A bladed tying tool that cuts feathers or fabric into wing shapes. Cutting is normally done on a soft pad to prevent dulling the blade. Usually, wing cutters are available in different sizes and have replaceable blades.

Wing maker
A tying tool, invented by George Leonard Herter, in the form of a small table and combs that forms fly wings

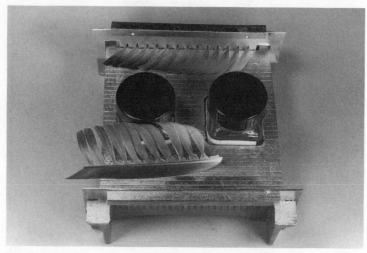

The Herter wing maker and completed wing panel.

from whole quills. Two combs, one for small wings and one for large wings, divide the barbs into wings. The wing butts are sealed with a drop of cement before removing from the wing maker.

Wing pad
The underdeveloped wing nodule of an immature insect; the imitation of such on an artificial pattern; the wing pods or buds; the covering or case over the developing wings of an insect. The forewing pad may cover the hind-wing pad and both may extend over the first and second abdominal segments. Wing pads darken to dark brown or black as the nymph attains maturity.

Witter (hook making)
In hook making, the hook *barb*. "When the barb or witter may be raised with the knife, taking care not to cut too deep" (James Rennie, *Alphabet of Angling* [1849]). Compare the word *whittle* (to cut or shave a thin slice).

Woven hackle
Tyer Franz Bernard Pott—the legendary fly tyer of Missoula, Montana—popularized the woven hackle and woven body in the 1920s and 1930s. His first patent in 1925 dealt principally with the woven "rock worm" body, but

Woven and trimmed ox-ear hair hackle.

the woven hackle was mentioned. His 1934 patent combined the woven body with a woven hackle, though the hackling process received scant attention. Pott, originally a barber and wig maker, used his occupational skills in weaving coarse, stiff badger and ox-ear hairs on three thread strands. The woven hackle was then mounted and wrapped as standard hackle. The stiff hackles maintained their shape in the heavy, steep rivers of the American West. Furthermore, the stiff hackles revealed the fly body and minimized hang-ups. George Grant of Missoula furthered the woven legend by creating a two-thread hackle weave.

Wrest(e) (hook making)

A hook-bending tool illustrated in the *Treatyse*: "To subject (something) to a twisting movement; to turn or twist." Old English: *wræstan* = to twist. The wreste illustrated in the *Treatyse* appears tapered to accommodate various bend diameters. The wreste usually has a groove, slot, or notch that holds the barb or point while the wreste is rotated, thus forming the hook bend. A wreste may merely hold the point as the hook is "pulled" or drawn into shape.

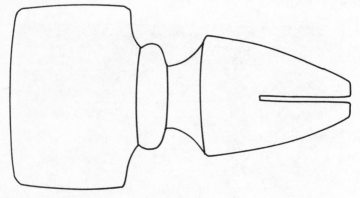

The wreste as illustrated in the *Treatyse*.

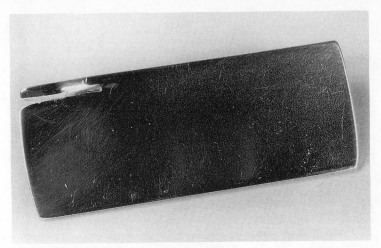

A modern plate wreste made by John Betts.

Wulff

A fly type usually characterized by hair wings and tail and a yarn body with various hackle colors. There are many variations on the Wulff clan, such as those that incorporate a yarn body and calf-tail wings. These viseless patterns were created in 1929 by Lee Wulff, who had studied engineering at Stanford University and art in Paris. The original Wulff pattern used bucktail wings and tail, angora wool body, and two long saddle hackles. "I had felt that a heavy-bodied, large fly—I used flies tied on #10 hooks mostly—would be more attractive to the trout than the slim-bodied, small patterns of the day. The trout would be able to see it from a greater depth, and it would seem to them like a bigger mouthful and something that was worth coming up for" (Lee Wulff, *Lee Wulff on Flies* [1985]).

X-designation (X-rating)

The X-designation is a method of measuring leader terminals and tippets. The X-designation is derived, in part, from the gut sizing (see *Gut*). As a result of the uniform material (nylon) used in the manufacture of leaders and tippets, various formulas have evolved. With modern developments, the breaking strength of the X-designation has increased and probably will continue to increase. The dimensions, however, have not. At present, the breaking strength of a standard 8X (the finer diameter) is approximately 2 pounds; the breaking strength of 1X (the thicker diameter) is about 15 pounds. Storage, age, and knots all affect the breaking strength.

There are two rules for the X-designation—the *rule of eleven* and the *rule of four*. To determine the X-designation of a tippet (or leader), the angler applies the rule of eleven. Subtract the tippet decimal designation (fractions of an inch) from the number eleven. First, convert the thousandths designation to a single number: thus, a six-thousandths diameter (0.006) becomes 6. To find the

X-rating, subtract 6 from 11. In this example, the X-rating is 5 or 5X. If diameters ever become metric, then a new formula will have to be developed. The rule of four "matches" the hook size to the tippet by multiplying the X-rating by four. "Match" means that the tippet will have the rigidity to push the pattern out, yet be soft or supple enough to create a natural float. A 3X tippet = 3. 3 X 4 = 12. Thus a 3X tippet matches a size 12 hook. It is possible to select one hook size smaller or larger than indicated. A sparsely dressed size 10 and a fully dressed size 14 match the impedance (the resistance) of a balanced tippet and pattern. To determine the tippet size for a particular hook size, merely divide the hook size by the number 4. A size 12 hook divided by 4 equals 3; hence, a 3X tippet matches a size 12 hook. The smaller the hook size becomes, the less critical matching becomes: The impedance difference between a size 20 and a size 26 is negligible.

York bend (hook bend)

The York bend, a term introduced by Daiichi Hooks USA, describes a mildly curved hook shank that makes a continuous and subtle transition into the bend. The flowing meld of shank and bend provides realistic imitations, especially for terrestrials (such as grasshoppers) and nymphs (such as stoneflies and damselflies).

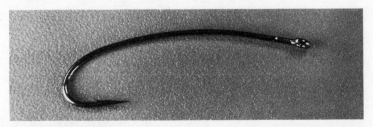

The York bend hook

Yorkshire Flybody hooks

A hook shape, manufactured by Partridge & Sons of Redditch, characterized by the rear extension of the eye wire so as to form a "detached" body. The hook was de-

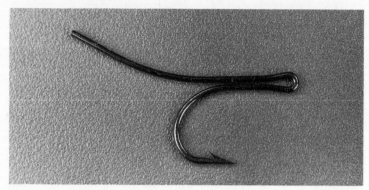

The looped shank of the Yorkshire Flybody hook forms the eye and the extended body. The extra wire makes this a relatively heavy hook for the size.

veloped by Peter Mackenzie-Philps of Yorkshire in 1973. The hook is available only in size 12 ("the large dayfly"), size 14 ("the dayfly"), and size 16 ("the midge").

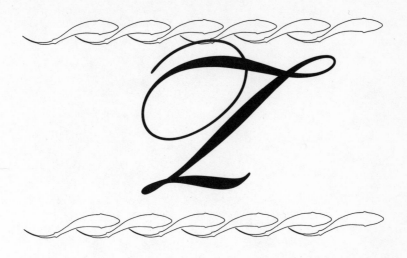

Z-twist

Z-twist indicates the direction of the twist of tying threads. The middle line (or diagonal) of the letter Z indicates the twist direction of the strand or strands of a vertical thread. Most tying threads have a slight or modest Z-twist. See *S-twist*.

The Z-twist   The S-twist

Bibliography

Please note that the following references may not be first editions.

Aelian [Aelianus, Claudius]. *On the Characteristics of Animals [De Natura Animalium]* vol. III, books XII–XVII. Translated by A. F. Scholfield. Cambridge, Mass.: Harvard University Press, 1959.

Aldam, W. H. *A Quaint Treatise on Flees, and the Art of Artyfichall Flee Making.* London, 1876.

Bainbridge, George C. *The Fly Fisher's Guide, Illustrated by Coloured Plates Representing Upwords of Forty of the Most Useful Flies Accurately Copied from Nature.* Based on the Liverpool, 1816 first edition. The Fly Fisher's Classic Library, 1992.

Bainbridge, W. G. *The Fly-Fisher's Guide to Aquatic Flies and Their Imitation.* London: A & C Black Ltd., 1936.

Bark, Conrad Voss. *A History of Fly Fishing.* Ludlow: Merlin Unwin Books, 1992.

Barnes [Berners], Dame Juliana (attributed author). *An Older Form of the Treatyse of Fysshynge Wyth an Angle,* printed from the Alfred Denison manuscript. Preface and glossary by Thomas Satchell. London: W. Satchell & Company, 1883.

Bernard, J. *Fly-Dressing.* London: Herbert Jenkins Limited, 1932.

Berners, Dame Juliana (attributed author). *The Book of Saint Albans.* Includes facsimile reprint of *The Treatyse of Fysshynge Wyth an Angle* (1496). New York: Abercrombie & Fitch, 1966.

Best, Thomas. *The Art of Angling,* 11th ed. London: T. C. Hansard, 1822.

Bickerdyke, John. *The Book of the All-Round Angler,* 7th rev. ed. London: Bazaar Exchange & Mart Office, ca. 1899.

Blacker, William. *The Art of Fly-Making, Angling and Dyeing of Colours,* 2d ed. London: George Nichols, Earl's Court, 1855.

Blades, William F. *Fishing Flies and Fly Tying,* rev. ed. Harrisburg, Pa.: Stackpole Company, 1962.

Bowlker, Charles. *The Art of Angling.* Ludlow: Richard Jones, 1839.

Boyle, Robert and Dave Whitlock. *The Second Fly-Tyer's Almanac.* Philadelphia: J. B. Lippincott Company, 1978.

Burgess, J. T. *Angling and How to Angle.* Revised by R. B. Marston. London: Frederick Warne & Company, 1895.

Burrard, Sir Gerald. *Fly-Tying: Principles & Practice,* 2d ed. London: Herbert Jenkins, Ltd., 1945.

Caucci, Al and Bob Nastasi. *Hatches II,* rev. ed. New York: Lyons & Burford, 1986.

Chaytor, A. H. *Letters to a Salmon Fisher's Son.* 1910.

Chetham, James. *The Angler's Vade Mecum,* 3d ed. London: William Battersby, 1700.

Cholmondeley-Pennell, H. *Fishing: Salmon and Trout,* 2d ed. London: Longmans, Green and Company, 1886.

Clarke, Brian, and John Goddard. *The Trout and the Fly.* New York: Nick Lyons Books, 1981.

Cummins, K. W. and R. W. Merritt, eds. *An Introduction to the Aquatic Insects of North America.* Dubuque: Kendall/Hunt Publishing Co., 1978.

Cutcliffe, H. C. *The Art of Trout Fishing on Rapid Streams.* London: Sampson Low, Marston, Searle & Rivington, 1863.

Darbee, Harry with Austin Mac Francis. *Catskill Flytier.* New York: J. B. Lippincott Company, 1977.

Davy, Sir Humphry. *Salmonia,* 5th ed. London: John Murray, 1869.

de Bergara, Juan. *El Manuscrito de Astorga.* Denmark: Gullanders Bogtrykkeri a-s, Skjern, "Flyleaves." Modern reprint, 1984.

Dennys, John (J. D.). *The Secrets of Angling. Augmented with Many Approved Experiments* by W. Lawson. Reprint of John Harrison, 1652 edition. London: Reprinted for Robert Triphook, 1811.

Diez, Jesus Pariente. *La Pesca de la Trucha en Los Rios Leoneses.* Argentina: Editorial Nebrija, S.A., 1979.

Donne, John. *Donne's Poetical Works.* Edited by H. J. C. Grierson. London: Lowe's & Brydone Printers, Ltd., 1953.

Dunne, J. W. *Sunshine and the Dry Fly.* London: A & C Black, Ltd., 1924.

Elder, Frank. *The Book of the Hackle.* Edinburgh: R & R Clark, 1979.

[Fitzgibbon, Edward.] Ephemera. *A Handbook of Angling.* London: Longman, Brown, Green & Longmans, 1848.

Foster, David. *The Scientific Angler,* 6th English ed., compiled by his sons. London: Bemrose & Sons, Ltd., ca. late 19th century.

Francis, Francis. *A Book on Angling,* 4th ed. London: Longmans, Green and Company, 1876.

Garrow-Green, G. *Trout Fishing in Brooks.* London: George Routledge & Sons, Ltd., ca. 1920.

Goddard, John. *The Super Flies of Still Water.* London: Ernest Benn, Ltd., 1977.

Hale, J. H. *How to Tie Salmon Flies,* 3d ed. London: Fishing Gazette, 1930.

Halford, Frederic M. *The Dry-Fly Man's Handbook.* London: George Routledge & Sons, Ltd., 1913.

Halford, Frederic M. *Floating Flies and How to Dress Them.* London: Sampson Low, Marston, Searle and Rivington, 1886.

Halford, Frederic M. *Modern Development of the Dry Fly.* Boston: Houghton, Mifflin & Company, 1923.

Hanna, Thomas J. *Fly-Fishing in Ireland.* London: H. F. & G. Witherby, 1933.

Harding, E. W. *The Flyfisher & the Trout's Point of View.* London: Seeley Service & Company, Ltd., 1931.

Harris, J. R. *An Angler's Entomology.* New York: A. S. Barnes & Co., 1939.

Hawksworth, David. *British Poultry Standards.* London: Butterworth Scientific, 1982.

Heacox, Cecil E. *The Compleat Brown Trout.* New York: Winchester Press, 1974.

Henn, T. R. *Practical Fly-Tying.* London: Adam & Charles Black, 1950.

Herter, George Leonard. *Professional Fly Tying, Spinning and Tackle Making: Manual and Manufacturers' Guide,* 19th ed. Waseca, Minn.: Herter's Inc., 1971.

Hewitt, Edward Ringwood. *Telling on the Trout.* New York: Charles Scribner's Sons, 1926.

Hills, John Waller. *A History of Fly Fishing for Trout.* New York: Freshet Press, 1971.

Hills, John Waller. *River Keeper: The Life of William James Lunn.* London: Geoffrey Bles, 1934.

Hills, John Waller. *A Summer on the Test.* London: Geoffrey Bles, 1946.

Hoffmann, Richard C. *Fisher's Craft & Lettered Art: Tracts on Fishing from the End of the Middle Ages.* Toronto: University of Toronto Press, 1997.

Hofland, T. C. *The British Angler's Manual.* Revised and enlarged by E. Jesse. London: H. G. Bohn, 1848.

Hunter, W. A. *Fisherman's Knots & Wrinkles,* 2d ed. London: A & C Black, Ltd., 1928.

Jackson, John. *The Practical Fly-Fisher,* 4th ed. London: Gibbings & Company, 1899.

Jackson, W. S. *Notes of a Fly Fisher: An Attempt at a Grammar of the Art.* London: The Fishing Gazette, Ltd., 1933.

Jennings, Preston J. *A Book of Trout Flies.* New York: Derrydale Press, 1935.

Jorgensen, Paul. *Salmon Flies.* Harrisburg, Penn. Stackpole Books, 1978.

Kelson, George. *The Salmon Fly: How to Dress It and How to Use It.* London, 1895.

Koch, Ed. *Fishing the Midge.* New York: Freshet Press, Inc., 1972.

La Branche, George M. L. *The Dry Fly and Fast Water.* New York: Charles Scribner's Sons, 1922.

Lane, Joscelyn. *Fly-Fisher's Pie.* London: Herbert Jenkins, Ltd., 1956.

Lane, Joscelyn. *Lake & Loch Fishing for Trout.* London: Seeley, Service & Company, 1954.

Lawrie, W. H. *All-Fur Flies & How to Dress Them.* London: Pelham Books, Ltd., 1967.

Lawrie, W. H. *A Reference Book of English Trout Flies*. London: Pelham Books, Ltd., 1967.

Lawrie, W. H. *Scottish Trout Flies: An Analysis and Compendium*. London: Frederick Muller, Ltd., 1966.

Leisenring, James E. and Vernon S. Hidy. *The Art of Tying the Wet Fly & Fishing the Flymph*. New York: Crown Publishers, Inc., 1971.

Leiser, Eric. *The Book of Fly Patterns*. New York: Alfred A. Knopf, 1987.

Leonard, J. Edson. *Flies*. New York: A. S. Barnes, 1960.

MacKay, Charles. *Lost Beauties of the English Language*. London: Bibliophile Books, 1987.

Malone, E. J. *Irish Trout and Salmon Flies*. Gerrards Cross: Colin Smythe Limited, 1984.

Mansfield, Kenneth, ed. *The Art of Angling* (3 vol.). London: Caxton Publishing Company, Limited, 1960.

Marbury, Mary Orvis. *Favorite Flies and Their History,* 2d ed. Boston: Houghton Mifflin, 1892.

March, J. *The Jolly Angler,* 4th ed. London: J. March, ca. 1842.

Marinaro, Vincent. *A Modern Dry-Fly Code*. New York: Nick Lyons Books, 1970.

Marinaro, Vincent. *In the Ring of the Rise*. New York: Crown Publishers, Inc., 1976.

Maunsell, G. W. *The Fisherman's Vade Mecum,* 3d ed. London: Adam & Charles Black, 1952.

Maxtone, Jamie Maxtone, ed. *The Best of Hardy's Anglers' Guides*. Midlothian, Scot.: MacDonald Publishers, 1982.

McClane, A. J., ed. *McClane's Standard Fishing Encyclopedia*. New York: Holt, Rinehart and Winston, 1965.

McClelland, H. G. *How to Tie Flies for Trout*. London: *Fishing Gazette,* 1939.

McClelland, H. G. *The Trout Fly Dresser's Cabinet of Devices,* 7th ed. London: *The Fishing Gazette, Ltd.*, 1931.

McCully, C. B. *A Book of Words: Fly Fishing*. Manchester, England: Carcanet Press Limited, 1992.

McDonald, John. *The Origins of Angling*. New York: Doubleday & Company, 1963.

Merwin, John, ed. *Stillwater Trout*. New York: Nick Lyons Books, 1980.

Mottram, J. C. *Fly-Fishing: Some New Arts and Mysteries*. London: The Field & Queen (Horace Cox), Ltd., 1915.

Mosely, Martin E. *The Dry-Fly Fisherman's Entomology*. London: George Routledge & Sons, Ltd., 1932.

Nemes, Sylvester. *The Soft-Hackled Fly*. Old Greenwich, Conn.: Chatham Press, 1975.

Niven, Richard. *The British Angler's Lexicon*. London: Sampson Low, Marston & Company, 1892.

Nonnos, Panopolitanus. *Dionysiaca, vol. III*. Translated by W. H. D. Rouse. Cambridge, Mass.: Harvard University Press, 1963.

Norris, Thaddeus. *The American Angler's Book, memorial ed*. Philadelphia: Porter & Coates, 1865.

Ogden, James. *Ogden on Fly Tying,* 3d ed. London: Sampson Low, Marston, Searle & Rivington, 1887.

O'Gorman, James. *The Practice of Angling Particularly as Regards Ire-land.* Reprint of the first edition, 1845. The Fly Fisher's Classic Library Edition. Bath, England: Bath Press Limited, 1993.

Onions, C. T., ed. *The Shorter Oxford English Dictionary.* Oxford: Clarendon Press, 1973.

Pain, Ernest C. *Fifty Years on the Test.* London: Phillip Allan, 1934.

Partridge, Eric. *Origins: A Short Etymological Dictionary of Modern English.* New York: Greenwich House, 1983.

Pequegnot, Jean-Paul. *French Fishing Flies.* New York: Nick Lyons Books, 1987.

Price, S. D. (Taff). *Rough Stream Trout Flies.* London: Adam and Charles Black, 1976.

Pritt, T. E. *North-Country Flies,* 2d ed. London: Sampson Low, Marston, Searle & Rivington, 1886.

Proper, Datus. *What the Trout Said.* New York: Alfred A. Knopf, Inc., 1982.

Pryce-Tannatt, T. E. *How to Dress Salmon Flies.* London: Adam and Charles Black, 1914.

Pulman, G. P. R. *The Vade Mecum of Fly-Fishing for Trout,* 3d ed. London: Longman, Brown, Green and Longmans, 1851.

Radcliffe, William. *Fishing from the Earliest Times.* Unchanged reprint of the London, 1921 edition. Chicago: Ares Publishing Inc., 1974.

Rennie, James. *Alphabet of Angling,* 3d ed. London: Henry G. Bohn, 1849.

Rhead, Louis. *American Trout Stream Insects.* New York: Frederick A. Stokes Company, 1916.

Ronalds, Alfred. *The Fly-Fisher's Entomology,* 3d ed. London: Longman, Brown, Green and Longmans, 1844.

Rosborough, E. H. "Polly." *Tying and Fishing the Fuzzy Nymph.* Manchester, Vt.: The Orvis Company, Inc., 1969.

Sandeman, Fraser. *By Hook and By Crook,* 2d ed. London: Henry Sotheran & Company, 1894.

Sheringham, H. T. *Elements of Angling.* London: Horace Cox, 1908.

Shipley, Joseph T. *Dictionary of Early English.* N.J.: Littlefield, Adams & Company, 1968.

Skues, G. E. M. *Minor Tactics of the Chalk Stream.* London: Adam and Charles Black, 1910.

Skues, G. E. M. *Side-Lines, Side-Lights & Reflections,* first American ed. Philadelphia: J. B. Lippincott Company, undated.

Skues, G. E. M. *Silk, Fur and Feather: The Trout-Fly Dresser's Year.* Beckenham, Kent: The Fishing Gazette, Ltd., 1950.

Skues, G. E. M. *The Way of a Trout with a Fly,* 3d ed. London: A & C Black, Ltd., 1935.

Smedley, Harold Hinsdill. *Fly Patterns and Their Origins,* 4th ed., rev. Muskegon, Mich.: Westshore Publications, 1950.

Stewart, W. C. *The Practical Angler.* Introduction and note by W. Earl Hodgson. London: A & C Black, Ltd., 1919.

Stoddart, Thomas Tod. *The Angler's Companion to the Rivers and Lochs of Scotland,* 2d ed. Edinburgh: William Blackwood and Sons, 1853.

Stratmann, Francis Henry. *A Middle-English Dictionary.* Based on first edition of 1891. London: Oxford University Press, 1967.

Sturgis, William B. *Fly-Tying.* New York: Charles Scribner's Sons, 1940.

Sturgis, William B. and Eric Taverner. *New Lines for Fly-Fishers.* London: Seeley, Service & Company, Ltd., 1946.

Sweet, Henry. *The Student's Dictionary of Anglo-Saxon.* Oxford: Clarendon Press, 1963.

Swisher, Doug and Carl Richards. *Emergers.* New York: Lyons & Burford, 1991.

Swisher, Doug and Carl Richards. *Selective Trout.* New York: Crown Publishers, Inc., 1971.

Talleur, Dick. *The Versatile Fly Tyer.* New York: Lyons & Burford, 1990.

Taylor, Samuel. *Angling in All Its Branches.* London: Longman & Rees, 1800.

Taverner, Eric. *Fly-Tying for Salmon.* London: Seeley Service & Company, Ltd., 1942.

Taverner, Eric. *Fly-Tying for Trout.* London: Seeley Service & Company, Ltd., 1939.

Taverner, Eric. *Trout Fishing from All Angles.* London: Seeley, Service & Company, Ltd., 1933.

Theakson, Michael. *British Angling Flies.* England: Ripon, 1883.

Tod, E. M. *Wet-Fly Fishing: Treated Methodically,* 3d ed. London: Sampson Low, Marston & Company, Ltd., 1914.

Venables, Col. Robert. *The Experienced Angler.* Reprint of Richard Marriot 1662 edition. London: T. Gosden, 1827.

Veniard, John. *Fly Dresser's Guide.* Illustrated by Donald Downs. London: A & C Black, 1972.

Wade, Henry. *Halcyon.* London, 1861.

Walker, C. F. *Fly-Tying as an Art.* London: Herbert Jenkins, Ltd., 1957.

Walker, Charles Edward. *Old Flies in New Dresses.* London: Lawrence and Bullen, Ltd., 1898.

Walton, Izaak and Charles Cotton. *The Complete Angler,* 2d Hawkins ed. London: John Hawkins of Twickenham, 1766.

Webster, David. *The Angler and the Loop-Rod.* Edinburgh: William Blackwood and Sons, 1885.

West, Leonard. *The Natural Trout Fly and Its Imitation.* Liverpool: William Potter, 1921.

Williams, A. Courtney. *A Dictionary of Trout Flies,* 5th ed. London: Adam & Charles Black, Ltd., 1982.

Williamson, Captain T. *The Complete Angler's Vade Mecum.* London: B. McMillam, 1808.

Woolley, Roger. *Modern Trout Fly Dressing.* London: Fishing Gazette, 1932.

Wulff, Lee. *Lee Wulff on Flies.* Harrisburg, Pa.: Stackpole Books, 1985.

Wuff, Lee. "The Wulff Fly Patterns." *Roundtable,* January/February, 1979.

Young, Paul H. *Making and Using the Fly and Leader,* 2d ed. Detroit: Paul Young, 1935.